TExES

Mathematics/Science
4-8 (114) Part 1 of 2

SECRETS

Study Guide
Your Key to Exam Success

TExES Test Review for the
Texas Examinations of Educator Standards

Dear Future Exam Success Story:

Congratulations on your purchase of our study guide. Our goal in writing our study guide was to cover the content on the test, as well as provide insight into typical test taking mistakes and how to overcome them.

Standardized tests are a key component of being successful, which only increases the importance of doing well in the high-pressure high-stakes environment of test day. How well you do on this test will have a significant impact on your future, and we have the research and practical advice to help you execute on test day.

The product you're reading now is designed to exploit weaknesses in the test itself, and help you avoid the most common errors test takers frequently make.

How to use this study guide

We don't want to waste your time. Our study guide is fast-paced and fluff-free. We suggest going through it a number of times, as repetition is an important part of learning new information and concepts.

First, read through the study guide completely to get a feel for the content and organization. Read the general success strategies first, and then proceed to the content sections. Each tip has been carefully selected for its effectiveness.

Second, read through the study guide again, and take notes in the margins and highlight those sections where you may have a particular weakness.

Finally, bring the manual with you on test day and study it before the exam begins.

Your success is our success

We would be delighted to hear about your success. Send us an email and tell us your story. Thanks for your business and we wish you continued success.

Sincerely,

Mometrix Test Preparation Team

Need more help? Check out our flashcards at: http://MometrixFlashcards.com/TExES

TABLE OF CONTENTS

Top 20 Test Taking Tips

1. Carefully follow all the test registration procedures
2. Know the test directions, duration, topics, question types, how many questions
3. Setup a flexible study schedule at least 3-4 weeks before test day
4. Study during the time of day you are most alert, relaxed, and stress free
5. Maximize your learning style; visual learner use visual study aids, auditory learner use auditory study aids
6. Focus on your weakest knowledge base
7. Find a study partner to review with and help clarify questions
8. Practice, practice, practice
9. Get a good night's sleep; don't try to cram the night before the test
10. Eat a well balanced meal
11. Know the exact physical location of the testing site; drive the route to the site prior to test day
12. Bring a set of ear plugs; the testing center could be noisy
13. Wear comfortable, loose fitting, layered clothing to the testing center; prepare for it to be either cold or hot during the test
14. Bring at least 2 current forms of ID to the testing center
15. Arrive to the test early; be prepared to wait and be patient
16. Eliminate the obviously wrong answer choices, then guess the first remaining choice
17. Pace yourself; don't rush, but keep working and move on if you get stuck
18. Maintain a positive attitude even if the test is going poorly
19. Keep your first answer unless you are positive it is wrong
20. Check your work, don't make a careless mistake

Number Concepts

Kinds of numbers

Natural numbers
Counting numbers, beginning with 1. (1, 2, 3, ...)

Whole numbers
Zero and the natural numbers. (0, 1, 2, ...)

Integers
The positive and negative values of the whole numbers. (-1, 0, 1, ...)

Rational number
Any number that can be expressed as a fraction with an integer as the numerator, and a non-zero integer as the denominator.

Irrational number
Any non-terminating, non-repeating number that CANNOT be expressed as a fraction. For example, π.

Real numbers
The set of all numbers that fall into any of the above categories.

Complex number
Any number that contains the imaginary number i, where $i^2 = -1$ and $= \sqrt{-1}$.

Adding and subtracting signed numbers

Addition: If the signs are the same, add the absolute values of the addends and apply the original sign to the sum. If the signs are different, take the absolute values of the addends and subtract the smaller value from the larger value. Apply the original sign of the number with the greater absolute value to the difference.

Subtraction: Change the sign of the number after the minus symbol and then follow the rules for addition.

Multiplying and dividing signed numbers

Multiplication: If the multiplicand and multiplier have the same sign, either both positive or both negative, the product is positive. If the multiplicand and multiplier have opposite signs, the product is negative. When there are more than two factors multiplied together, count the number of negative factors. If there are an odd number of negative factors, the product is negative. If there are an even number of factors, the product is positive. If zero is a factor, the answer is zero.

Division: If the dividend and divisor have the same sign, the quotient is positive. If the dividend and divisor have opposite signs, the quotient is negative. If the dividend is zero, the answer is zero, unless the divisor is also zero. Any time the divisor is zero, the quotient is undefined.

Numeric problems

Solve inside any parentheses first; solve exponents second. Then do all multiplication and division in the order they appear, from left to right. Finally, do all addition and subtraction in the order they appear, from left to right.

Field properties for addition and multiplication

Additive Identity
$a + 0 = a; 0 + a = a$

Additive Inverse
$a + (-a) = 0; (-a) + a = 0$

Associative
$(a + b) + c = a + (b + c)$ for addition and $(ab)c = a(bc)$ for multiplication

Closure
In addition, $a + b$ is a real number. In multiplication, ab is a real number.

Commutative
$a + b = b + a$ for addition and $ab = ba$ for multiplication.

Distributive
$a(b + c) = ab + ac$ and $(a + b)c = ac + bc$

Multiplicative Identity
$a \cdot 1 = a$ and $1 \cdot a = a$

Multiplicative Inverse
$a \cdot a^{-1} = 1$ and $a^{-1} \cdot a = 1$

Field properties for subtraction and division

Subtraction
$a - b = a + (-b)$

Division
$$a \div b = \frac{a}{b} = a \cdot b^{-1} = a \cdot \frac{1}{b}$$

Properties of natural numbers

Prime
Counting numbers greater than 1 whose only factors are 1 and itself.

Composite
Counting numbers greater than 1 that are not prime.

Note: 1 is neither prime nor composite; 2 is the only prime even number.

Prime Factorization
According to the Fundamental Theorem of Arithmetic, every composite number can be uniquely written as the product of prime numbers.

Greatest Common Factor (gcf)
The greatest number that will divide evenly into each of two or more natural numbers. To find the gcf, factor each number and identify each common prime factor the least number of times it appears in any one of the natural numbers in the set. Find the product of the identified common prime factors. If there no common factors, the gcf is 1.

Greatest Common Divisor (gcd)
Signified by gcd(m, n), where m and n are both natural numbers, it is the same as the greatest common factor.

Least Common Multiple (lcm)
Signified by lcm(m, n), where m and n are both natural numbers, it is the lowest number that is a multiple of each of the natural numbers in the set. To find the lcm, factor each natural number and identify each common prime factor the most number of times it appears in any one of the natural numbers in the set. Find the product of the identified common prime factors.

Finding GCF

The greatest common factor of a group of algebraic expressions may be a monomial or a polynomial. Begin by factoring all the algebraic expressions until each expression is represented as a group of factors consisting of monomials and prime polynomials. To find the greatest common factor, take each monomial or polynomial that appear as a factor in every algebraic expression and multiply. This will give you a polynomial with the largest numerical coefficient and largest degree that is a factor of the given algebraic expressions.

Ratio, proportion, and cross products

Ratio: A comparison of two quantities; expressed in one of three ways: a to b; a:b; or $\frac{a}{b}$. The units in both terms must be identical to have a correct ratio. If it is not possible to convert to the same units, write the expression as a rate, such as miles per hour, or miles/hour.

Proportion: A statement of two equal ratios, such as $\frac{a}{b} = \frac{c}{d}$.

- 4 -

Cross Products: In a proportion, it is the product of the numerator of the first ratio multiplied by the denominator of the second ratio, and the denominator of the first ratio multiplied by the numerator of the second ratio, or $\frac{a}{b} = \frac{c}{d} \Rightarrow ad = bc$. In a true proportion, the cross products will always be equal.

Percent

Percent means "hundredth" or "per hundred." To change a percent to a decimal, divide the number by 100. This is accomplished by moving the decimal point two places to the left. The percent of an amount, P, is the percentage rate, R, times the whole amount, or base, B. In other words, $P = RB$. To write a percent as a proportion, use the formula $\frac{R}{100} = \frac{\text{partial amount}}{\text{whole amount}}$.

Mean and weighted mean

Mean: The same thing as the arithmetic average. Use the formula
$$\text{mean} = \frac{\text{sum of all numbers in the set}}{\text{quantity of numbers in the set}}$$

Weighted mean: Weighted values, such as $w_1, w_2, w_3, \ldots$ are assigned to each member of the set $x_1, x_2, x_3, \ldots$. Use the formula
$$\text{weighted mean} = \frac{w_1 x_1 + w_2 x_2 + w_3 x_3 + \cdots + w_n x_n}{w_1 + w_2 + w_3 + \cdots + w_n}$$

Make sure there is one weighted value for each member of the set.

Monomials and polynomials

Monomial: A single constant, variable, or product of constants and variables, such as $2, x, 2x$, or $\frac{2}{x}$. There will never be addition or subtraction symbols in a monomial. Like monomials have like variables, but they may have different coefficients.

Polynomial: An algebraic expression which uses addition and subtraction to combine two or more monomials. Two terms make a binomial; three terms make a trinomial.

Degree of a Monomial: The sum of the exponents of the variables.

Degree of a Polynomial: The highest degree of any individual term.

Patterns of special products

Perfect Trinomial Squares
$x^2 + 2xy + y^2 = (x + y)^2$ or $x^2 - 2xy + y^2 = (x - y)^2$

Difference Between Two Squares
$x^2 - y^2 = (x + y)(x - y)$

Sum of Two Cubes
$$x^3 + y^3 = (x + y)(x^2 - xy + y^2)$$
Note: the second factor is NOT the same as a perfect trinomial square, so do not try to factor it further.

Difference Between Two Cubes

$$x^3 - y^3 = (x - y)(x^2 + xy + y^2)$$

Again, the second factor is NOT the same as a perfect trinomial square.

Perfect Cubes
$$x^3 + 3x^2y + 3xy^2 + y^3 = (x + y)^3 \text{ and } x^3 - 3x^2y + 3xy^2 - y^3 = (x - y)^3$$

Multiplying two binomials

First: Multiply the first term of each binomial
Outer: Multiply the outer terms of the binomials
Inner: Multiply the inner terms of the binomials
Last: Multiply the last term of each binomial
$$(Ax + By)(Cx + Dy) = ACx^2 + ADxy + BCxy + BDy^2$$

Dividing polynomials

Set up a long division problem, dividing a polynomial by either a monomial or another polynomial of equal or lesser degree. When dividing by a monomial, divide each term of the polynomial by the monomial.

When dividing a polynomial by a polynomial, begin by arranging the terms of each polynomial in order of one variable. You may arrange in ascending or descending order, but be consistent with both polynomials. To get the first term of the quotient, divide the first term of the dividend by the first term of the divisor. Multiply the first term of the quotient by the entire divisor and subtract that product from the dividend. Repeat for the second and successive terms until you either get a remainder of zero or a remainder whose degree is less than the degree of the divisor. If the quotient has a remainder, write the answer as a mixed expression in the form
$\text{quotient} + \frac{\text{remainder}}{\text{divisor}}$.

Factoring polynomials

First, check for a common monomial factor. When the greatest common monomial factor has been factored out, look for patterns of special products: differences of two squares, the sum or difference of two cubes for binomial factors, or perfect trinomial squares for trinomial factors. If the factor is a trinomial but not a perfect trinomial square, look for a factorable form, such as:
$$x^2 + (a + b)x + ab = (x + a)(x + b) \text{ or } (ac)x^2 + (ad + bc)x + bd = (ax + b)(cx + d).$$

- 6 -

For factors with four terms, look for groups to factor. Once you have found the factors, write the original polynomial as the product of all the factors. Make sure all of the polynomial factors are prime. Monomial factors may be prime or composite. Check your work by multiplying the factors to make sure you get the original polynomial.

Rational expressions

Rational Expression: A fraction with polynomials in both the numerator and the denominator; the value of the polynomial in the denominator cannot be equal to zero.

To add or subtract rational expressions, first find the common denominator, then rewrite each fraction as an equivalent fraction with the common denominator. Finally, add or subtract the numerators to get the numerator of the answer, and keep the common denominator as the denominator of the answer.

When multiplying rational expressions, factor each polynomial and cancel like factors (a factor which appears in both the numerator and the denominator). Then, multiply all remaining factors in the numerator to get the numerator of the product, and multiply the remaining factors in the denominator to get the denominator of the product. Remember – cancel entire factors, not individual terms.

To divide rational expressions, take the reciprocal of the divisor (the rational expression you are dividing by) and multiply by the dividend.

Complex fractions

Complex Fraction: A fraction that contains a fraction in its numerator, denominator, or both. Simplify it by rewriting it as a division problem, or multiply both the numerator and denominator by the least common denominator of the fractions in the complex fraction.

Square root

Square Root: A number which, when multiplied by itself, yields a real number. Positive real numbers have exactly one real positive n^{th} root, and n could be even or odd. Every real number has exactly one real n^{th} root when n is odd. Negative numbers only have real n^{th} roots if n is odd.

Working with exponents

A positive integer exponent indicates the number of times the base is multiplied by itself. Anything raised to the zero power is equal to 1. A negative integer exponent means you must take the reciprocal of the result of the corresponding positive integer exponent. A fractional exponent signifies a root. The following formulas all apply to exponents:

$$x^0 = 1$$
$$x^{-n} = \frac{1}{x^n}$$
$$\left(\frac{a}{b}\right)^{-1} = \frac{b}{a}$$
$$(x^a)^b = x^{ab}$$
$$(xy)^n = x^n y^n$$
$$\left(\frac{x}{y}\right)^n = \frac{x^n}{y^n}$$

0^0 is undefined.

Terms relative to equations

Equation: Shows that two mathematical expressions are equal; may be true or false.

One Variable Linear Equation: An equation written in the form $ax + b = 0$, where $a \neq 0$.

Root: A solution of an equation; a number that makes the equation true when it is substituted for the variable.

Solution Set: The set of all solutions of an equation.

Identity: A term whose value or determinant is equal to 1.

Empty Set: A situation in which an equation has no true solution.

Equivalent Equations: Equations with identical solution sets.

Absolute value

Absolute Value: The distance a number is from zero; always a positive number or zero. The absolute value of a number, x, is written $|x|$.

Inequalities

Inequality: A mathematical statement showing that two mathematical expressions are not equal. Inequalities use the > (greater than) and < (less than) symbols rather than the equal sign. Graphs of the solution set of inequalities are represented on a number line. Open circles are used to show that an equation approaches a number but is never equal to that number.

Conditional inequality: An inequality that has certain values for the variable that will make the condition true, and other values for the variable that will make the condition false.

- 8 -

Absolute inequality: An inequality that can have any real number as the value for the variable to make the condition true, and no real number value for the variable that will make the condition false.

To solve an inequality, follow the same rules as solving an equation. However, when multiplying or dividing an inequality by a negative number, you must reverse the direction of the inequality sign.

Double Inequality: A situation in which two inequality statements apply to the same variable expression.

When working with absolute values in inequalities, apply the following rules:

$$|ax + b| < c \Rightarrow -c < ax + b < c$$

$$|ax + b| > c \Rightarrow ax + b < -c \text{ or } ax + b > c$$

One-variable quadratic equations

One-Variable Quadratic Equation: An equation that can be written in the form $x^2 + bx + c = 0$, where a, b, and c are the coefficients. This is also known as the standard form of an equation.

The solutions of quadratic equations are called roots. A quadratic equation may have one real root, two different real roots, or no real roots. The roots can be found using one of three methods: factoring, completing the square, or using the quadratic formula.

Any time you are solving a quadratic equation, never divide both sides by the variable or any expression containing the variable. You are at risk of dividing by zero if you do, thus getting an extraneous, or invalid, root.

Completing the square root

To complete the square, rewrite the equation so that all terms containing the variable are on the left side of the equal sign, and all the constants are on the right side of the equal sign. Make sure the coefficient of the squared term is 1. If there is a coefficient with the squared term, divide each term on both sides of the equal side by that number. Next, work with the coefficient of the single-variable term. Square half of this coefficient, and add that value to both sides. Now you can factor the left side (the side containing the variable) as the square of a binomial. $x^2 + 2ax + a^2 = C \Rightarrow (x + a)^2 = C$, where x is the variable, and a and C are constants. Take the square root of both sides and solve for the variable. Substitute the value of the variable in the original problem to check your work.

Quadratic formula

The quadratic formula is used to solve quadratic equations when other methods are more difficult. To use the quadratic formula to solve a quadratic equation, begin by rewriting the equation in standard form $ax^2 + bx + c = 0$, where a, b, and c are coefficients. Once you have identified the values of the coefficients, substitute those values into the quadratic formula $= \frac{-b \pm \sqrt{b^2 - 4ac}}{2a}$. Evaluate the equation and simplify the expression. Again, check each root by substituting into the original equation.

In the quadratic formula, the portion of the formula under the radical ($b^2 - 4ac$) is called the discriminant. If the discriminant is zero, there is only one root: zero. If the discriminant is positive, there are two different real roots. If the discriminant is negative, there are no real roots.

Systems of equations

System of Equations: A set of simultaneous equations that all use the same variables. A solution to a system of equations must be true for each equation in the system.

Consistent System: A system of equations that has at least one solution.

Inconsistent System: A system of equations that has no solution.

Systems of equations may be solved using one of four methods: substitution, elimination, transformation of the augmented matrix and using the trace feature on a graphing calculator.

Solving systems of two linear equations by substitution

To solve a system of linear equations by substitution, start with the easier equation and solve for one of the variables. Express this variable in terms of the other variable. Substitute this expression in the OTHER equation, and solve for the other variable. The solution should be expressed in the form (x, y). Substitute the values into both of the original equations to check your answer.

Solving systems of equations by elimination or addition

To solve a system of equations using elimination or addition, begin by rewriting both equations in standard form $Ax + By = C$. Check to see if the coefficients of one pair of like variables adds to zero. If not, multiply one or both of the equations by a non-zero number to make one set of like variables add to zero. Add the two equations to solve for one of the variables. Substitute this value into one of the original equations to solve for the other variable. Check your work by substituting into the other equation.

Trace feature of a graphing calculator

Using the trace feature on a calculator requires that you rewrite each equation, isolating the y-variable on one side of the equal sign. Enter both equations in the graphing calculator and plot the graphs simultaneously. Use the trace cursor to find where the two lines cross. Use the zoom feature if necessary to obtain more accurate results. Always check your answer by substituting into the original equations. The trace method is likely to be less accurate than other methods due to the resolution of graphing calculators, but is a useful tool to provide an approximate answer.

Graphing two-variable linear inequalities

Whenever you have an inequality using the symbol < or >, always use a dashed line for the graph. If the inequality uses the symbol ≤ or ≥ , use a solid line since equal is an option. All graphs of linear inequalities require that one side of the line is shaded. To determine which side to shade, select any point that is not on the line (the origin is an easy point to use if it is not on the line) and substitute the x- and y-values into the inequality. If the inequality is true, shade the side with that point. If the inequality is false, shade the other side of the line.

Intersect, coincident, and parallel

Intersect: Exactly one solution that satisfies both equations. It is represented by a single point where the two lines intersect on a graph.

Coincident: An infinite number of solutions that satisfy both equations. It is represented by a single line, since all points are in common for both linear equations.

Parallel: No solutions satisfy both equations. It is represented by parallel lines on the graph, since the lines never intersect.

Cartesian coordinate plane

The Cartesian coordinate plane consists of two number lines placed perpendicular to each other, and intersecting at the zero point, also known as the origin. The horizontal number line is known as the x-axis, with positive values to the right of the origin, and negative values to the left of the origin. The vertical number line is known as the y-axis, with positive values above the origin, and negative values below the origin. Any point on the plane can be identified by an ordered pair in the form (x,y), called coordinates. The x-value of the coordinate is called the abscissa, and the y-value of the coordinate is called the ordinate. The two number lines divide the plane into four quadrants: I, II, III, and IV.

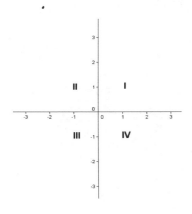

Line equations

Standard form
$Ax + By = C$; the slope is $\frac{-A}{B}$ and the y-intercept is $\frac{C}{B}$.

Slope-Intercept form

$y = mx + b$, where m is the slope and b is the y-intercept.

Point-Slope form

$y - y_1 = m(x - x_1)$, where m is the slope and (x_1, y_1) is a point on the line.

Two-Point form

$\frac{y - y_1}{x - x_1} = \frac{y_2 - y_1}{x_2 - x_1}$, where (x_1, y_1) and (x_2, y_2) are two points on the given line.

Intercept form

$\frac{x}{x_1} + \frac{y}{y_1} = 1$, where $(x_1, 0)$ is the point at which a line intersects the x-axis, and $(0, y_1)$ is the point at which the same line intersects the y-axis.

Parabola

The standard form of a parabola is $= ax^2 + bx + c$, where a, b, and c are coefficients and $a \neq 0$. In this form, if the value of a is positive, the parabola opens upward. If the value of a is negative, the parabola opens downward. The axis of symmetry is the line $= \frac{-b}{2a}$. The vertex of the parabola is the point $\left(\frac{-b}{2a}, \frac{4ac - b^2}{4a}\right)$.

The vertex form of a parabola is $= a(x - h)^2 + k$, where a, h, and k are coefficients. In this form, if the value of a is positive, the parabola open upward. If the value of a is negative, the parabola opens downward. The vertex of the parabola is the point (h, k).

Circle and sphere

The standard form of a circle is
$$(x - h)^2 + (y - k)^2 = r^2$$
where h, k, and r are coefficients. The center of the circle is the point (h, k), and the radius is r units.
The general equation of a sphere is

$$(x - a)^2 + (y - b)^2 + (z - c)^2 = r^2$$

where a, b, c, and r are coefficients. The center of the sphere is the point (a, b, c), and the radius is r units.

Ellipse

The standard form of an ellipse is $\frac{(x-h)^2}{a^2} + \frac{(y-k)^2}{b^2} = 1$, where a, b, h, and k are coefficients. The center of the ellipse is the point (h, k). The ellipse has four vertices at points $(h + a, k)$, $(h - a, k)$, $(h, k + b)$, and $(h, k - b)$. The ellipse has two lines of symmetry. The horizontal axis of symmetry is the line through points $(h + a, k)$ and $(h - a, k)$. The vertical axis of symmetry is the line through the points $(h, k + b)$ and $(h, k - b)$. When these lines are drawn, the longer axis is the major axis, and the shorter axis is the minor axis. The lengths of the two axes are given by $2|a|$ and $2|b|$. If $a^2 > b^2$, the ellipse will be longer in the x-direction. If $a^2 < b^2$, the ellipse will be longer in the y-direction.

Hyperbola

The hyperbola has two standard forms. The first standard form of a hyperbola is $\frac{(x-h)^2}{a^2} - \frac{(y-k)^2}{b^2} = 1$, where $a, b, h,$ and k are coefficients. The center of the hyperbola is the point (h, k), and it opens to the left and right along a line having the equation $y = k$. The vertices are the points $(h - a, k)$ and $(h + a, k)$. The asymptotes are lines which the hyperbola approaches but never reaches, and are defined by the equations $y = k + \frac{b}{a}(x - h)$ and $= k - \frac{b}{a}(x - h)$. The asymptotes are also described as the diagonals of a rectangle with center at the center of the hyperbola and legs of length $2|a|$ and $2|b|$.

The second standard form of a hyperbola is $\frac{(y-k)^2}{b^2} - \frac{(x-h)^2}{a^2} = 1$, where $a, b, h,$ and k are coefficients. The center of the hyperbola is the point (h, k), and it opens upward and downward along a line having the equation $x = h$. The vertices are the points $(h, k - b)$ and $(h, k + b)$. The asymptotes are lines which the hyperbola approaches but never reaches, and are defined by the equations $= k + \frac{a}{b}(x - h)$ and $y = k - \frac{a}{b}(x - h)$. The asymptotes are also described as the diagonals of a rectangle with center at the center of the hyperbola and legs of length $2|a|$ and $2|b|$.

Note that the only difference between the equation of an ellipse and the equation of a hyperbola is the symbol between the two fractions.

Slope, horizontal, vertical, parallel, and perpendicular

Slope: A ratio of the change in height to the change in horizontal distance. On a graph with two points (x_1, y_1) and (x_2, y_2), the slope is represented by the formula $m = \frac{y_2 - y_1}{x_2 - x_1}$; $x_1 \neq x_2$. If the value of the slope is positive, the line slopes upward from left to right. If the value of the slope is negative, the line slopes downward from left to right. If the y-coordinates are the same for both points, the slope is 0 and the line is a horizontal line. If the x-coordinates are the same for both points, there is no slope and the line is a vertical line.

Horizontal: Having a slope of zero. On a graph, a line that is the same distance from the x-axis at all points.

Vertical: Having no slope. On a graph, a line that is the same distance from the y-axis at all points.

Parallel: Lines that have equal slopes.

Perpendicular: Lines that have slopes that are negative reciprocals of each other: $\frac{a}{b}$ and $\frac{-b}{a}$.

Finding midpoint and distance of two points

To find the midpoint of two points (x_1, y_1) and (x_2, y_2), average the x-coordinates to get the x-coordinate of the midpoint, and average the y-coordinates to get the y-coordinate of the midpoint. The formula is

$$\text{midpoint} = \left(\frac{x_1 + x_2}{2}, \frac{y_1 + y_2}{2} \right)$$

The distance between two points is the same as the length of the hypotenuse of a right triangle with the two given points as endpoints, and the two sides of the right triangle parallel to the x-axis and y-axis, respectively. The length of the segment parallel to the x-axis is the difference between the x-coordinates of the two points. The length of the segment parallel to the y-axis is the difference between the y-coordinates of the two points. Use the Pythagorean Theorem $a^2 + b^2 = c^2$ or $c = \sqrt{a^2 + b^2}$ to find the distance. The formula is:

$$\text{distance} = \sqrt{(x_2 - x_1)^2 + (y_2 - y_1)^2}$$

Patterns and Algebra

Functions

A function is an equation that has exactly one value for y (the dependent variable) for each member of x (the independent variable). The set of all values for x is the domain of the function, and the set of all corresponding values of y is the range of the function. When looking at a graph of an equation, the easiest way to determine if the equation is a function or not is to conduct the vertical line test. If a vertical line drawn through any value of x crosses the graph in more than one place, the equation is not a function.

Properties of functions

In functions with the notation $f(x)$, the value substituted for x in the equation is called the argument. The domain is the set of all values for x in a function. Unless otherwise given, assume the domain is the set of real numbers that will yield real numbers for the range. This is the domain of definition.

The graph of a function is the set of all ordered pairs (x, y) that satisfy the equation of the function. The points that have zero as the value for y are called the zeros of the function. These are also the x-intercepts, because that is the point at which the graph crosses, or intercepts, the x-axis. The points that have zero as the value for x are the y-intercepts because that is where the graph crosses the y-axis.

Horizontal and vertical shift

Horizontal and vertical shift occur when values are added to or subtracted from the x or y values, respectively.

If a constant is added to the y portion of each point, the graph shifts up. If a constant is subtracted from the y portion of each point, the graph shifts down. This is represented by the expression $y = f(x) \pm k$, where k is a constant.

If a constant is added to the x portion of each point, the graph shifts left. If a constant is subtracted from the x portion of each point, the graph shifts right. This is represented by the expression $y = f(x \pm k)$, where k is a constant.

Stretch, shrink, and reflection

Stretching, shrinking, and reflecting occur when a function is multiplied by a constant. If the function is multiplied by a real number constant greater than 1, the graph is stretched. If a constant greater than 1 is multiplied by the x portion of each point, the graph is stretched horizontally. If a constant greater than 1 is multiplied by the y portion of each point, the graph is stretched vertically.

If the function is multiplied by a real number constant greater than zero but less than 1, the graph shrinks. If a positive real number constant less than 1 is multiplied by the x portion of each point, the graph shrinks horizontally. If a positive real number constant less than 1 is multiplied by the y portion of each point, the graph shrinks vertically.

If the x portion of each point is multiplied by a negative number, the graph is reflected across the x-axis. If the y portion of each point is multiplied by a negative number, the graph is reflected across the y-axis.

Exponential functions and logarithmic functions

Exponential functions are equations that have the format $y = b^x$, where base $b > 0$ and $b \neq 1$. The exponential function can also be written $f(x) = b^x$. Logarithmic functions are equations that have the format $y = \log_b x$ or $(x) = \log_b x$. The base b may be any number except one; however, the most common bases for logarithms are base 10 and base e, also known as the natural logarithm. On the test, any logarithm that does not have an assigned value of b is assumed to be base e. Exponential functions and logarithmic functions are related in that one is the inverse of the other. If $f(x) = b^x$, then $f^{-1}(x) = \log_b x$. Also, the equation $y = b^x$ is the same as $= \log_b y$.

The following properties apply to logarithmic expressions:

$$\log_b 1 = 0$$
$$\log_b b = 1$$
$$\log_b b^p = p$$
$$\log_b MN = \log_b M + \log_b N$$
$$\log_b \frac{M}{N} = \log_b M - \log_b N$$
$$\log_b M^p = p \log_b M$$

Linear functions

In a linear function, the rate of change (the slope) is constant throughout. Linear functions are straight line graphs and are used to describe things such as distance, where the *rate of change* does not change. The standard form of a linear equation is $Ax + By = C$, where A, B, and C are real numbers. Other forms of linear equations make solving problems easier. The slope-intercept form $y = mx + b$ (m and b are real numbers, m is the slope, $m \neq 0$, and b is the y-intercept) is useful for finding the zeros of the function. Solve the equation $mx + b = 0$ for x to get $= -\frac{b}{m}$, which is the only zero of the function. The domain and range are both the set of all real numbers.

Constant and identity functions

Constant functions are given by the equation $y = b$ or $f(x) = b$, where b is a real number. There is a single variable y in the equation, so there are no zeros unless $b = 0$, in which case every point is a zero. The graph of a constant function is a horizontal line of slope 0 that is positioned b units from the x-axis. If b is positive, the line is above the x-axis; if b is negative, the line is below the x-axis.

Identity functions are identified by the equation $y = x$ or $(x) = x$, where every value of y is equal to its corresponding value of x. The only zero is the point $(0, 0)$. The graph is a diagonal line with slope 1.

Quadratic function

A quadratic function follows the equation pattern $= ax^2 + bx + c$, or $f(x) = ax^2 + bx + c$, where a, b, and c are real numbers and $a \neq 0$. The domain of a quadratic function is the set of all real numbers. The range is also real numbers, but only those in the subset of the domain that satisfy the equation. To determine the number of roots of a quadratic equation, solve the expression $b^2 - 4ac$. If this value is positive, there are two unique real zeros. If this value equals zero, there is one root, which is a double root. If this value is less than zero, there are no real roots. To find the roots of a quadratic equation, solve the equation $x^2 + bx + c = 0$. In a quadratic function, the rate of change varies throughout, but there is a maximum or a minimum value for the amount of change. Quadratic functions are useful in determining things such as how changing the price of something will affect its sales and profit margin.

Graphs of quadratic functions

A quadratic function will always form a parabola when it is graphed. In the equation $(x) = ax^2 + bx + c$, if a is positive, the parabola will open upward. If a is negative, the parabola will open downward. The axis of symmetry is a vertical line that passes through the vertex. To determine whether or not a parabola will intersect the x-axis, check the number of real roots. An equation with two real roots will cross the x-axis twice. An equation with one real root will have its vertex on the x-axis. An equation with no real roots will not contact the x-axis.

Fundamental Theorem of Algebra and Remainder Theorem

The Fundamental Theorem of Algebra states that every function, when set equal to zero, has a solution, and that every polynomial has at least one root. Every polynomial will have as many roots as the largest integer exponent in the polynomial. For example, if x^4 is the largest exponent of a term, the polynomial will have exactly 4 roots. Some roots may be double roots, so those must be counted twice. The Fundamental Theorem of Algebra does allow for complex roots, so do not expect to find all real roots for every function.

The Remainder Theorem is useful for determining the remainder when a polynomial is divided by a binomial. The Remainder Theorem states that if a function $f(x)$ is divided by a binomial $x - a$, where a is a real number, the remainder will be the value of $f(a)$. If $f(a) = 0$, then a is a root of the polynomial at the point $(a, 0)$.

Factor Theorem and Rational Root Theorem

The Factor Theorem is related to the Remainder Theorem and states that if $f(a) = 0$ then $(x - a)$ is a factor of the function.

Rational Root Theorem: A function $f(x) = a_n x^n + a_{n-1} x^{n-1} + a_{n-2} x^{n-2} + \cdots + a_1 x + a_0$ with integral coefficients will have a rational root that, when reduced to lowest terms, will be a fraction such that the numerator is a factor of a_0 and the denominator is a factor of a_n.

The Rational Root Theorem also deals with complex roots. If a function has a complex root $p + qi$, where i is the imaginary number, then its conjugate, or $p - qi$, is also a root of the function.

One way to help determine approximations of roots is to evaluate functions with different values. If $f(p)$ and $f(q)$ have opposite signs, you know there must be a zero somewhere between those two numbers.

Rational functions

A rational function is a fraction such that $f(x) = \frac{p(x)}{q(x)}$, $p(x)$ and $q(x)$ are both polynomials and $q(x) \neq 0$. The domain is the set of all real numbers EXCEPT any number for which $q(x) = 0$. The range is the set of real numbers that satisfies the function when the domain is applied. Whenever you graph a rational function, you will have vertical asymptotes wherever $q(x) = 0$. If the polynomial in the numerator is of lesser degree than the polynomial in the denominator, the x-axis will also be a horizontal asymptote. If the numerator and denominator have equal degrees, there will be a horizontal asymptote not on the x-axis. If the degree of the numerator is exactly one greater than the degree of the denominator, the graph will have an oblique, or diagonal, asymptote.

Square root functions

A square root function is a function that contains a radical and is in the format $(x) = \sqrt{ax + b}$. The domain is the set of all real numbers that yields a positive radicand or a radicand equal to zero. Because square root values are assumed to be positive unless otherwise identified, the range is all real numbers from zero to infinity. To find the zero of a square root function, set the radicand equal to zero and solve for x. The graph of a square root function is always to the right of the zero and always above the x-axis.

Absolute value functions

An absolute value function is in the format $(x) = |ax + b|$. Like other functions, the domain is the set of all real numbers. However, because absolute value indicates positive numbers, the range is limited to positive real numbers. To find the zero of an absolute value function, set the portion inside the absolute value sign equal to zero and solve for x. An absolute value function is also known as a piecewise function because it must be solved in pieces – one for if the value inside the absolute value sign is positive, and one for if the value is negative. The function can be expressed as $f(x) = \begin{cases} ax + b & \text{if } ax + b \geq 0 \\ -(ax + b) & \text{if } ax + b < 0 \end{cases}$

This will allow for an accurate statement of the range.

Polynomial functions

A polynomial function is a function with multiple terms and multiple powers of x, such as
$$f(x) = a_n x^n + a_{n-1} x^{n-1} + a_{n-2} x^{n-2} + \cdots + a_1 x + a_0$$
where n is a positive integer that is the highest exponent in the polynomial, and $a_n \neq 0$. Like quadratic equations, the domain is the set of all real numbers. If the greatest exponent in the polynomial is even, the polynomial is said to be of even degree and the range is the set of real numbers that satisfy the function. If the greatest exponent in the polynomial is odd, the polynomial is said to be odd and the range, like the domain, is the set of all real numbers.

One-to-one functions

In a one-to-one function, each value of x has exactly one value for y (this is the definition of a function) *and* each value of y has exactly one value for x. While the vertical line test will determine if a graph is that of a function, the horizontal line test will determine if a function is a one-to-one function. If a horizontal line drawn at any value of y intersects the graph in more than one place, the graph is not that of a one-to-one function. Do not make the mistake of using the horizontal line test exclusively in determining if a graph is that of a one-to-one function. A one-to-one function must pass both the vertical line test and the horizontal line test.

Monotone, even, and odd functions, and discontinuities

A monotone function is a function whose graph either constantly increases or constantly decreases. Examples include the functions $(x) = x$, $f(x) = -x$, or $f(x) = x^3$.

An even function has a graph that is symmetric with respect to the y-axis and satisfies the equation $(x) = f(-x)$. Examples include the functions $f(x) = x^2$ and $(x) = ax^n$, where a is any real number and n is a positive even integer.

An odd function has a graph that is symmetric with respect to the origin and satisfies the equation $(x) = -f(-x)$. Examples include the functions $f(x) = x^3$ and $(x) = ax^n$, where a is any real number and n is a positive odd integer.

Any time there are vertical asymptotes or holes in a graph, such that the complete graph cannot be drawn as one continuous line, a graph is said to have discontinuities. Examples would include the graphs of hyperbolas that are functions, and the function f(x)=tan x.

Variables that vary directly and inversely

Variables that vary directly are those that either both increase at the same rate or both decrease at the same rate. For example, in the functions $f(x) = kx$ or $(x) = kx^n$, where k is a positive constant and $n > 0$, the value of y ($f(x)$) increases as the value of x increases and decreases as the value of x decreases.

Variables that vary inversely are those where one increases while the other decreases. For example, in the functions $f(x) = \frac{k}{x}$ or $f(x) = \frac{k}{x^n}$ where k is a positive constant, the value of y increases as the value of x decreases, and the value of y decreases as the value of x increases.

In both cases, k is constant of variation.

Algebraic and transcendental functions

Algebraic functions are those that exclusively use polynomials and roots. These would include polynomial functions, rational functions, square root functions, and all combinations of these functions, such as polynomials as the radicand. These combinations may be joined by addition, subtraction, multiplication, or division, but may not include variables as an exponent.

Transcendental functions are all functions that are non-algebraic. Any function that includes logarithms, trigonometric functions, variables as exponents, or any combination that includes any or all of these is not algebraic in nature, even if the function includes polynomials or roots, and therefore a transcendental function.

Equal functions

Equal functions are those whose domains are equal, and whose ranges are equal for all corresponding values in the domain. In other words, $f(x)$ and $g(x)$ are equal if every value of $f(x)$ is equal to every corresponding value of $g(x)$.

To find the sum of the functions f and g, assuming the ranges are all real numbers, solve each function individually and add the results: $(f + g)(x) = f(x) + g(x)$.

To find the difference of the functions f and g, assuming the ranges are all real numbers, solve each function individually and subtract the results: $(f - g)(x) = f(x) - g(x)$.

Product, quotient, and composite of two functions

To find the product of the functions f and g, assuming the ranges are all real numbers, solve each function individually and then multiply the results: $(f \cdot g)(x) = f(x) \cdot g(x)$. This is much easier, and less prone to mathematical error, than trying to multiply two polynomials together before applying the value of x.

To find the quotient of the functions f and g, assuming the ranges are all real numbers, solve each function individually and then divide the results: $\left(\frac{f}{g}\right)(x) = \frac{f(x)}{g(x)}$; $g(x) \neq 0$.

The composite of two functions f and g, represented by the symbol $(f \circ g)(x)$ or $f(g(x))$, is found by substituting $g(x)$ for all instances of x in $f(x)$ and simplifying. It is important to note that $(f \circ g)(x)$ does not always equal $(g \circ f)(x)$. The process is not commutative like addition or multiplication expressions. If $(f \circ g)(x)$ does equal $(g \circ f)(x)$, the two functions are inverses of each other. This is one of the easiest tests to determine if two functions are inverses. If the two functions are graphed, the graphs will be reflections of each other with respect to the line $y = x$.

Matrix

A matrix is an array of number arranged in columns and rows. A matrix that has exactly one column or exactly one row is a vector. A matrix with an equal number of columns and rows is called a square matrix. A matrix (plural matrices) is used to represent the coefficients of a system of linear equations and is useful in solving those systems. Each element of a matrix is a real or complex number, or may be an expression representing a real or complex number. A matrix is generally represented by a capital letter, with its elements represented by the corresponding lowercase letter with two subscripts indicating the row and column of the element. For example, n_{ab} represents the element n in row a column b of matrix N.

Matrix order

A matrix is described in terms of the number of rows and columns it contains in the format $a \times b$, where a is the number of rows and b is the number of columns. A matrix of order $1 \times b$ has 1 row with multiple elements. It is called a row vector of order b. A matrix of order $a \times 1$ has 1 column with multiple elements. It is called a column vector of order a. Any matrix of order $a \times b$ where $a = b$ is a square matrix.

It is important to note that graphing calculators (required for the test) have the capability of solving matrices. If you have enough memory in your calculator, you can enter a matrix of order up to 99×99, depending on the calculator.

Main diagonal

The main diagonal only applies to a square matrix. In this case, it is the elements found in a line from the top left corner to the bottom right corner of the square matrix. For example, a square matrix N of order 4 would have the elements n_{11}, n_{22}, n_{33}, and n_{44} as the main diagonal

$$\begin{bmatrix} n_{11} & n_{12} & n_{13} & n_{14} \\ n_{21} & n_{22} & n_{23} & n_{24} \\ n_{31} & n_{32} & n_{33} & n_{34} \\ n_{41} & n_{42} & n_{43} & n_{44} \end{bmatrix}$$

A matrix of order 5×4 would not have a main diagonal because no straight line between the top left corner and the bottom right corner that joins the elements.

$$\begin{bmatrix} n_{11} & n_{12} & n_{13} & n_{14} \\ n_{21} & n_{22} & n_{23} & n_{24} \\ n_{31} & n_{32} & n_{33} & n_{34} \\ n_{41} & n_{42} & n_{43} & n_{44} \\ n_{51} & n_{52} & n_{53} & n_{54} \end{bmatrix}$$

Diagonal, identity and zero matrix

A diagonal matrix is a square matrix that has a zero for every element in the matrix except the elements on the main diagonal. All the elements on the main diagonal must be nonzero numbers.

$$\begin{bmatrix} 2 & 0 & 0 & 0 \\ 0 & 3 & 0 & 0 \\ 0 & 0 & 4 & 0 \\ 0 & 0 & 0 & 5 \end{bmatrix}$$

If every element on the main diagonal of a diagonal matrix is equal to one, the matrix is also called an identity matrix.

$$\begin{bmatrix} 1 & 0 & 0 & 0 \\ 0 & 1 & 0 & 0 \\ 0 & 0 & 1 & 0 \\ 0 & 0 & 0 & 1 \end{bmatrix}$$

A zero matrix is a matrix that has zero as the value for every element in the matrix.

$$\begin{bmatrix} 0 & 0 & 0 & 0 \\ 0 & 0 & 0 & 0 \\ 0 & 0 & 0 & 0 \\ 0 & 0 & 0 & 0 \end{bmatrix}$$

The zero matrix is the *identity for matrix addition*. Do not confuse the zero matrix with the identity matrix.

Negative and equal matrix

The negative of a matrix is also known as the additive inverse of a matrix. If matrix N is the given matrix, then matrix $-N$ is its negative. This means that every element n_{ab} is equal to $-n_{ab}$ in the negative. To find the negative of a given matrix, change the sign of every element in the matrix and keep all elements in their original corresponding positions in the matrix.

If two matrices have the same order and all corresponding elements in the two matrices are the same, then the two matrices are equal matrices.

Transposing a matrix

A matrix N may be transposed to matrix N^T by changing all rows into columns and changing all columns into rows. The easiest way to accomplish this is to swap the positions of the row and column notations for each element. For example, suppose the element in the second row of the third column of matrix N is $n_{23} = 4$. In the transposed matrix N^T, the transposed element would be $n_{32} = 4$, and it would be placed in the third row of the second column. To quickly transpose a matrix by hand, begin with the first column and rewrite a new matrix with those same elements in the same order in the first row. Write the elements from the second column of the original matrix in the second row of the transposed matrix. Continue this process until all columns have been completed. If the original matrix is identical to the transposed matrix, the matrices are symmetric.

Scalar and scalar product

Like any other situation in mathematics, a scalar is simply a number or a numerical amount. To find the scalar product of a matrix of any order, multiply each element of the original matrix by the scalar to get the element of the new matrix. The new matrix is of the same order as the original matrix, and each element, multiplied by the scalar, is placed in its corresponding position in the matrix. Follow this pattern when finding the scalar product of a matrix:

$$k \begin{bmatrix} n_{11} & n_{12} & n_{13} & n_{14} \\ n_{21} & n_{22} & n_{23} & n_{24} \\ n_{31} & n_{32} & n_{33} & n_{34} \\ n_{41} & n_{42} & n_{43} & n_{44} \end{bmatrix} = \begin{bmatrix} kn_{11} & kn_{12} & kn_{13} & kn_{14} \\ kn_{21} & kn_{22} & kn_{23} & kn_{24} \\ kn_{31} & kn_{32} & kn_{33} & kn_{34} \\ kn_{41} & kn_{42} & kn_{43} & kn_{44} \end{bmatrix}$$

Adding matrices and additive identity element

When adding matrices, the matrices must all be of the same order. To find the sum of two matrices of the same order, add the values of the corresponding elements and place the sum in the corresponding position of the new matrix. For all matrices, the additive identity element is the zero matrix. Adding zero to any number will not change the value of the number, and adding a zero matrix to any matrix of the same order will not change the value of the matrix. Follow this pattern when finding the sum of two matrices of the same order:

$$\begin{bmatrix} m_{11} & m_{12} \\ m_{21} & m_{22} \end{bmatrix} + \begin{bmatrix} n_{11} & n_{12} \\ n_{21} & n_{22} \end{bmatrix} = \begin{bmatrix} m_{11} + n_{11} & m_{12} + n_{12} \\ m_{21} + n_{21} & m_{22} + n_{22} \end{bmatrix}$$

Subtracting matrices and additive inverse

To find the difference between two matrices of the same order, find the negative of the second matrix and add it to the first matrix, following the rules of addition for matrices. Alternately, you can subtract each element of the second matrix from its corresponding element in the first matrix and write the difference in the corresponding position of the resulting matrix. For all matrices of the same order, the additive inverse is the negative of the original matrix. Follow this pattern when finding the difference between two matrices of the same order:

$$\begin{bmatrix} m_{11} & m_{12} \\ m_{21} & m_{22} \end{bmatrix} - \begin{bmatrix} n_{11} & n_{12} \\ n_{21} & n_{22} \end{bmatrix} = \begin{bmatrix} m_{11} - n_{11} & m_{12} - n_{12} \\ m_{21} - n_{21} & m_{22} - n_{22} \end{bmatrix}$$

Conformable matrices

Matrices that have the same order are called conformable matrices for matrix addition or matrix subtraction. For all addition and subtraction of matrices, the matrices involved must be conformable. There is no definition of addition or subtraction of matrices in any situation involving non-conformable matrices. For all conformable matrices, you can complete the addition of matrices on your graphing calculator with the addition key. To complete the subtraction of conformable matrices on your graphing calculator, you may have to first find the additive inverse of the second matrix and then use the addition feature to solve it as the sum of two conformable matrices.

Unlike conformable matrices for addition or subtraction, conformable matrices for multiplication must have the number of columns in the first matrix equal to the number of rows in the second matrix. The second matrix is considered to be premultiplied by the first matrix, and the first matrix is said to be postmultiplied by the second matrix. If the number of columns in the first matrix does not equal the number of rows in the second matrix, then the matrices are not conformable and the multiplication process is not defined. It is important to note that the commutative principle of multiplication does not apply to the multiplication of matrices.

Linear product vectors

The linear product, also referred to as the dot product, of two vectors is the sum of the products of the corresponding elements of the two vectors. To find the linear product, the first vector MUST be a row vector, and the second vector MUST be a column vector with an equal number of elements. Find the product of the first element in each vector, as well as the product of each subsequent pair of elements until each corresponding pair has been multiplied. Finally, find the sum of the products. Follow this pattern to find the linear product of two vectors:

$$[m_{11} \quad m_{12} \quad m_{13}] \cdot \begin{bmatrix} n_{11} \\ n_{21} \\ n_{31} \end{bmatrix} = m_{11}n_{11} + m_{12}n_{21} + m_{13}n_{31}$$

Linear product of matrices

To find the linear product of two matrices, the number of columns in the first matrix must equal the number of rows in the second matrix. The two matrices do not have to be of the same order as long as this condition is met. The resulting matrix will be a matrix of order equal to the number of rows in the first matrix and the number of columns in the second matrix. To multiply matrices, treat each row and column as individual vectors and follow the pattern for multiplying vectors. In the new matrix, the answer from multiplying the first row vector by the first column vector is the element positioned at the intersection of the first row, first column of the new matrix. The answer from multiplying the second row vector by the first column vector is the element positioned at the intersection of the second row, first column of the new matrix. Continue this pattern until each row of the first matrix has been multiplied by each column of the second vector.

$$\begin{bmatrix} m_{11} & m_{12} \\ m_{21} & m_{22} \\ m_{31} & m_{32} \end{bmatrix} \times \begin{bmatrix} n_{11} & n_{12} & n_{13} \\ n_{21} & n_{22} & n_{23} \end{bmatrix}$$

$$= \begin{bmatrix} m_{11}n_{11} + m_{12}n_{21} & m_{11}n_{12} + m_{12}n_{22} & m_{11}n_{13} + m_{12}n_{23} \\ m_{21}n_{11} + m_{22}n_{21} & m_{21}n_{12} + m_{22}n_{22} & m_{21}n_{13} + m_{22}n_{23} \\ m_{31}n_{11} + m_{32}n_{21} & m_{31}n_{12} + m_{32}n_{22} & m_{31}n_{13} + m_{32}n_{23} \end{bmatrix}$$

Inverse of a 2x2 matrix

The inverse of matrix M is matrix N, such that $MN = NM$. In this case, matrix M and matrix N must both be square matrices of equal order. It is important to note that just because a matrix is a square matrix does not mean that matrix will have an inverse. If a square matrix does have an inverse, the inverse is unique to that square matrix, and the matrix is considered to be nonsingular. For any matrix M that has an inverse, the inverse is represented by the symbol M^{-1}. To calculate the inverse of a 2×2 square matrix, use the following pattern:

$$\begin{bmatrix} m_{11} & m_{12} \\ m_{21} & m_{22} \end{bmatrix}^{-1} = \begin{bmatrix} \dfrac{m_{22}}{\Delta} & \dfrac{-m_{12}}{\Delta} \\ \dfrac{-m_{21}}{\Delta} & \dfrac{m_{11}}{\Delta} \end{bmatrix}, \text{ where } \Delta = m_{11}m_{22} - m_{12}m_{21} \neq 0.$$

Determinant

A determinant is a scalar value that is determined by a function of a square matrix. The scalar value Δ obtained from a 2×2 square matrix $\begin{bmatrix} m_{11} & m_{12} \\ m_{21} & m_{22} \end{bmatrix}$ according to the formula $\Delta = m_{11}m_{22} - m_{12}m_{21} \neq 0$ is called the determinant of the matrix. The determinant of matrix N is denoted $\det(N)$ or $|N|$. To find the determinant of a 3×3 square matrix, follow the pattern below:

$$\det \begin{bmatrix} a & b & c \\ d & e & f \\ g & h & i \end{bmatrix} = aei + bfg + cdh - ceg - bdi - afh$$

Beyond a 3×3 matrix, the process for finding the determinant becomes cumbersome. Use your graphing calculator, converting decimals to fractions, if necessary.

Partitioned matrix

A partitioned matrix is matrix that has been divided, or partitioned, into square matrices. The individual square matrices may or may not be of the same order. Partitioned matrices can be used to find the inverses of nonsingular matrices. For example, given the 2×2 nonsingular matrix $N = \begin{bmatrix} a & b \\ c & d \end{bmatrix}$, you can find the inverse N^{-1} by creating a partitioned matrix, where the first partition is the original square matrix, and the second partition is the 2×2 identity matrix as follows: $\begin{bmatrix} a & b & | & 1 & 0 \\ c & d & | & 0 & 1 \end{bmatrix}$. To find the inverse of the original 2×2 matrix, perform elementary row operations, such as multiplying a row by a nonzero scalar, adding two rows, interchanging two rows, or a combination of these, to convert the partition on the left to an identity matrix. The result is that the partition on the right will be the inverse of the original matrix.

ransformation of an augmented matrix

The transformation of an augmented matrix is a process useful for solving systems of equations. When a system of equations is not easily solvable using normal algebraic procedures, use the transformation of an augmented matrix to find the solution, if it exists. If there is a solution, the system is consistent. If there is no solution, the system is inconsistent. Begin by arranging each equation of the system in the format $ax + by + cz = d$. Write the system of equations in the correct format, numbering the coefficients with subscripts as follows:

$$a_{11}x + b_{12}y + c_{13}z = d_1$$
$$a_{21}x + b_{22}y + c_{23}z = d_2$$
$$a_{31}x + b_{32}y + c_{33}z = d_3$$

Enter each coefficient into its corresponding position in the augmented matrix as follows:

$$\begin{matrix} a_{11} & b_{12} & c_{13} & d_1 \\ a_{21} & b_{22} & c_{23} & d_2 \\ a_{31} & b_{32} & c_{33} & d_3 \end{matrix}$$

To solve the augmented matrix and the system of equations, use the elementary row operations to form an identity matrix. If an identity matrix is not possible, get the augmented matrix as close as possible. If all but the last column forms an identity matrix, the values in the last column are the solutions to the system of equations, with $d_1 = x$, $d_2 = y$, and $d_3 = z$. If one or more rows of the identity matrix are incomplete, the solution is not a unique solution.

Reduced row-echelon forms

When a system of equations has a solution, finding the transformation of the augmented matrix will result in one of three reduced row-echelon forms. Only one of these forms will give a unique solution to the system of equations, however. Use the following formats and formulas to get the solutions to a system of equations:

$$\begin{bmatrix} 1 & 0 & 0 & x_0 \\ 0 & 1 & 0 & y_0 \\ 0 & 0 & 1 & z_0 \end{bmatrix}$$ gives the unique solution $x = x_0;\ y = y_0;\ z = z_0$

$$\begin{bmatrix} 1 & 0 & k_1 & x_0 \\ 0 & 1 & k_2 & y_0 \\ 0 & 0 & 0 & 0 \end{bmatrix}$$ gives a non-unique solution $x = x_0 - k_1 z;\ y = y_0 - k_2 z$

$$\begin{bmatrix} 1 & j_1 & k_1 & x_0 \\ 0 & 0 & 0 & 0 \\ 0 & 0 & 0 & 0 \end{bmatrix}$$ gives a non-unique solution $x = x_0 - j_1 y - k_1 z$

Reduced row-echelon forms can be used to solve systems of equations with more variables, but the process is extremely time-consuming. Use your graphing calculator to solve the system for you.

Determinant of a 3x3 matrix

Finding the determinant of a 3×3 matrix requires the use of multiple 2×2 determinants. Multiply the value in the first row, first column, by the value of the 2×2 determinant formed when the first row and first column are removed. Subtract the product of the value in the first row, second column, and the 2×2 determinant formed when the first row and second column are removed. Add the product of the value in the first row, third column, and the 2×2 determinant formed when the first row and third column are removed. The general pattern is as follows:

$$\begin{vmatrix} a_{11} & a_{12} & a_{13} \\ a_{21} & a_{22} & a_{23} \\ a_{31} & a_{32} & a_{33} \end{vmatrix} = a_{11} \begin{vmatrix} a_{22} & a_{23} \\ a_{32} & a_{33} \end{vmatrix} - a_{12} \begin{vmatrix} a_{21} & a_{23} \\ a_{31} & a_{33} \end{vmatrix} + a_{13} \begin{vmatrix} a_{21} & a_{22} \\ a_{31} & a_{32} \end{vmatrix}$$

Inverse matrix

To determine whether or not a matrix has an inverse, first consider the shape of the matrix. If the matrix is not a square matrix, it does not have an inverse. If the matrix is a square matrix of any order, find the determinant of the matrix. If the determinant is equal to zero, the matrix does not have an inverse. If the determinant is anything except zero, the matrix has an inverse. Keep in mind that if a square matrix has any row or column with all values in that row or column equal to zero, then the value of the matrix is equal to zero and there is no inverse.

Geometric transformations

The four geometric transformations are translations, reflections, rotations, and dilations. When geometric transformations are expressed as matrices, the process of performing the transformations is simplified. For calculations of the geometric transformations of a planar figure, make a $2 \times n$ matrix, where n is the number of vertices in the planar figure. Each column represents the rectangular coordinates of one vertex of the figure, with the top row containing the values of the x-coordinates and the bottom row containing the values of the y-coordinates. For example, given a planar triangular figure with coordinates (x_1, y_1), (x_2, y_2), and (x_3, y_3), the corresponding matrix is $\begin{bmatrix} x_1 & x_2 & x_3 \\ y_1 & y_2 & y_3 \end{bmatrix}$. You can then perform the necessary transformations on this matrix to determine the coordinates of the resulting figure.

Translation of a planar figure

A translation moves a figure along the x-axis, the y-axis, or both axes without changing the size or shape of the figure. To calculate the new coordinates of a planar figure following a translation, set up a matrix of the coordinates and a matrix of the translation values and add the two matrices.

$$\begin{bmatrix} h & h & h \\ v & v & v \end{bmatrix} + \begin{bmatrix} x_1 & x_2 & x_3 \\ y_1 & y_2 & y_3 \end{bmatrix} = \begin{bmatrix} h + x_1 & h + x_2 & h + x_3 \\ v + y_1 & v + y_2 & v + y_3 \end{bmatrix}$$

where h is the number of units the figure is moved along the x-axis (horizontally) and v is the number of units the figure is moved along the y-axis (vertically).

Reflection of a planar figure

$y = x$

To find the reflection of a planar figure over the x-axis, set up a matrix of the coordinates of the vertices and pre-multiply the matrix by the 2×2 matrix $\begin{bmatrix} 1 & 0 \\ 0 & -1 \end{bmatrix}$ so that $\begin{bmatrix} 1 & 0 \\ 0 & -1 \end{bmatrix}\begin{bmatrix} x_1 & x_2 & x_3 \\ y_1 & y_2 & y_3 \end{bmatrix} = \begin{bmatrix} x_1 & x_2 & x_3 \\ -y_1 & -y_2 & -y_3 \end{bmatrix}$. To find the reflection of a planar figure over the y-axis, set up a matrix of the coordinates of the vertices and pre-multiply the matrix by the 2×2 matrix $\begin{bmatrix} -1 & 0 \\ 0 & 1 \end{bmatrix}$ so that $\begin{bmatrix} -1 & 0 \\ 0 & 1 \end{bmatrix}\begin{bmatrix} x_1 & x_2 & x_3 \\ y_1 & y_2 & y_3 \end{bmatrix} = \begin{bmatrix} -x_1 & -x_2 & -x_3 \\ y_1 & y_2 & y_3 \end{bmatrix}$. To find the reflection of a planar figure over the line $y = x$, set up a matrix of the coordinates of the vertices and pre-multiply the matrix by the 2×2 matrix $\begin{bmatrix} 0 & 1 \\ 1 & 0 \end{bmatrix}$ so that $\begin{bmatrix} 0 & 1 \\ 1 & 0 \end{bmatrix}\begin{bmatrix} x_1 & x_2 & x_3 \\ y_1 & y_2 & y_3 \end{bmatrix} = \begin{bmatrix} y_1 & y_2 & y_3 \\ x_1 & x_2 & x_3 \end{bmatrix}$. Remember that the order of multiplication is important when multiplying matrices. The commutative property does not apply.

Rotation of a planar figure

To find the coordinates of the figure formed by rotating a planar figure about the origin θ degrees in a counterclockwise direction, set up a matrix of the coordinates of the vertices and pre-multiply the matrix by the 2×2 matrix $\begin{bmatrix} \cos\theta & \sin\theta \\ -\sin\theta & \cos\theta \end{bmatrix}$. For example, if you want to rotate a figure 90º clockwise around the origin, you would have to convert the degree measure to 270º counterclockwise and solve the 2×2 matrix you have set as the pre-multiplier: $\begin{bmatrix} \cos 270° & \sin 270° \\ -\sin 270° & \cos 270° \end{bmatrix} = \begin{bmatrix} 0 & -1 \\ 1 & 0 \end{bmatrix}$. Use this as the pre-multiplier for the matrix $\begin{bmatrix} x_1 & x_2 & x_3 \\ y_1 & y_2 & y_3 \end{bmatrix}$ and solve to find the new coordinates.

Dilation of a planar figure

To find the dilation of a planar figure by a scale factor of k, set up a matrix of the coordinates of the vertices of the planar figure and pre-multiply the matrix by the 2×2 matrix $\begin{bmatrix} k & 0 \\ 0 & k \end{bmatrix}$ so that $\begin{bmatrix} k & 0 \\ 0 & k \end{bmatrix}\begin{bmatrix} x_1 & x_2 & x_3 \\ y_1 & y_2 & y_3 \end{bmatrix} = \begin{bmatrix} kx_1 & kx_2 & kx_3 \\ ky_1 & ky_2 & ky_3 \end{bmatrix}$. In this case, k will be positive if the figure is being enlarged, and negative if the figure is being shrunk. Again, remember that when multiplying matrices, the order of the matrices is important. The commutative principle does not apply, and the matrix with the coordinates of the figure must be the second matrix.

Geometry and Measurement

Altitude, height, concurrent, and orthocenter

Altitude of a Triangle: A line segment drawn from one vertex perpendicular to the opposite side. In the diagram below, $\overline{BE}$, $\overline{AD}$, and $\overline{CF}$ are altitudes.

Height of a Triangle: The length of the altitude, although the two terms are often used interchangeably.

Concurrent: Lines that intersect at one point. In a triangle, the three altitudes are concurrent.

Orthocenter of a Triangle: The point of concurrency of the altitudes of a triangle. Note that in an obtuse triangle, the orthocenter will be outside the circle, and in a right triangle, the orthocenter is the vertex of the right angle.

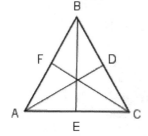

Median and centroid

Median of a Triangle: A line segment drawn from one vertex to the midpoint of the opposite side. This is not the same as the altitude, except the altitude to the base of an isosceles triangle and all three altitudes of an equilateral triangle. Centroid of a Triangle: The point of concurrency of the medians of a triangle. This is the same point as the orthocenter only in an equilateral triangle. Unlike the orthocenter, the centroid is always inside the triangle. The centroid can also be considered the exact center of the triangle. Any shape triangle can be perfectly balanced on a tip placed at the centroid. The centroid is also the point that is two-thirds the distance from the vertex to the opposite side.

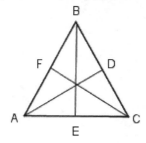

Perpendicular and angle bisectors

Perpendicular bisector: A line that bisects the side of a triangle at a right angle. The perpendicular bisectors of a triangle are concurrent at a point called the circumcenter that is equidistant from the three vertices. The circumcenter is also the center of the circle that can be circumscribed about the triangle.

Angle bisector: A line that divides the vertex angle of a triangle into two equal parts. The angle bisectors are concurrent at a point called the incenter that is equidistant from the three sides. The incenter is also the center of the largest circle that can be inscribed in the triangle.

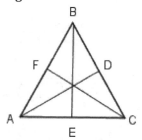

Congruent and similar figures

Congruent figures are geometric figures that have the same size and shape. All corresponding angles are equal, and all corresponding sides are equal. It is indicated by the symbol ≅.

Congruent polygons

Similar figures are geometric figures that have the same shape, but do not necessarily have the same size. All corresponding angles are equal, and all corresponding sides are proportional, but they do not have to be equal. It is indicated by the symbol ~.

 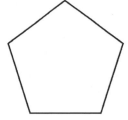

Similar polygons

Note that all congruent figures are also similar, but not all similar figures are congruent.

Symmetry, symmetric, and line of symmetry

Line of Symmetry: The line that divides a figure or object into two symmetric parts. Each symmetric half is congruent to the other. An object may have no lines of symmetry, one line of symmetry, or more than one line of symmetry.

No lines of symmetry   One line of symmetry   More than one line of symmetry

Quadrilaterals, parallelograms, and trapezoids

Quadrilateral: A closed two-dimensional geometric figure comprised of exactly four straight sides. The sum of the interior angles of any quadrilateral is 360°.

Parallelogram: A quadrilateral that has exactly two pairs of opposite parallel sides. The sides that are parallel are also congruent. The opposite interior angles are always congruent, and the consecutive interior angles are supplementary. The diagonals of a parallelogram bisect each other. Each diagonal divides the parallelogram into two congruent triangles.

Trapezoid: Traditionally, a quadrilateral that has exactly one pair of parallel sides. Some math texts define trapezoid as a quadrilateral that has at least one pair of parallel sides. Because there are no rules governing the second pair of sides, there are no rules that apply to the properties of the diagonals of a trapezoid.

Rectangles, rhombuses, and squares

Rectangles, rhombuses, and squares are all special forms of parallelograms.

Rectangle: A parallelogram with four right angles. All rectangles are parallelograms, but not all parallelograms are rectangles. The diagonals of a rectangle are congruent.

Rhombus: A parallelogram with four congruent sides. All rhombuses are parallelograms, but not all parallelograms are rhombuses. The diagonals of a rhombus are perpendicular to each other.

Square: A parallelogram with four right angles and four congruent sides. All squares are also parallelograms, rhombuses, and rectangles. The diagonals of a square are congruent and perpendicular to each other.

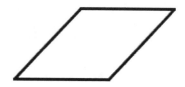

Ray, angle, and vertex

A ray is a portion of a line extending from a point in one direction. It has a definite beginning, but no ending. Rays are represented by the symbol $\rightarrow$

An angle is formed when two rays meet at a common point. It may be a common starting point, or it may be the intersection of rays, lines, and/or line segments. Angles are represented by the symbol $\angle$

The vertex is the point at which the two rays meet to form an angle. If the angle is formed by intersecting rays, lines, and/or line segments, the vertex is the point at which four angles meet. The opposite angles are called vertical angles, and their measures are equal.

Types of angles

An acute is an angle with a degree measure less than 90º.

A right angle is an angle with a degree measure of exactly 90º.

An obtuse angle is an angle with a degree measure greater than 90º but less than 180º.

A straight angle is an angle with a degree measure of exactly 180º. This is also a semicircle.

A reflex angle is an angle with a degree measure greater than 180º but less than 360º.

A full angle is an angle with a degree measure of exactly 360°. This is also a circle.

Complementary, supplementary, and adjacent angles

Complementary: Two angles whose sum is exactly 90°. The two angles may or may not be adjacent. In a right triangle, the two acute angles are complementary.

Supplementary: Two angles whose sum is exactly 180°. The two angles may or may not be adjacent. Two intersecting lines always form two pairs of supplementary angles. Adjacent supplementary angles will always form a straight line.

Adjacent: Two angles that have the same vertex and share a side. Vertical angles are not adjacent because they share a vertex but no common side.

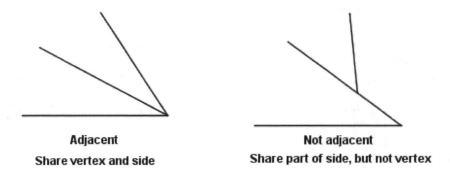

Adjacent
Share vertex and side

Not adjacent
Share part of side, but not vertex

Plane

A plane is a two-dimensional flat surface defined by three non-collinear points. A plane extends an infinite distance in all directions in those two dimensions. It contains an infinite number of points, parallel lines and segments, intersecting lines and segments, as well as parallel or intersecting rays. A plane will never contain a three-dimensional figure or skew lines.

A plane may intersect a circular conic surface, such as a cone, to form conic sections, such as the parabola, hyperbola, circle or ellipse.

Two given planes will either be parallel or they will intersect to form a line.

Intersecting lines, parallel lines, vertical angles, and transversals

Intersecting Lines: Lines that have exactly one point in common.

Parallel Lines: Lines in the same plane that have no points in common and never meet. It is possible for lines to be in different planes, have no points in common, and never meet, but they are not parallel because they are in different planes.

Vertical Angles: Non-adjacent angles formed when two lines intersect. Vertical angles are congruent. In the diagram, $\angle ABD \cong \angle CBE$ and $\angle ABC \cong \angle DBE$.

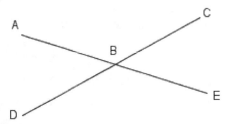

Transversal: A straight line that intersects at least two other lines, which may or may not be parallel.

Interior angles, exterior angles, and corresponding angles

Interior Angles: When two parallel lines are cut by a transversal, the angles that are between the two parallel lines are interior angles. In the diagram below, angles 3, 4, 5, and 6 are interior angles.

Exterior Angles: When two parallel lines are cut by a transversal, the angles that are outside the parallel lines are exterior angles. In the diagram below, angles 1, 2, 7, and 8 are exterior angles.

Corresponding Angles: When two parallel lines are cut by a transversal, the angles that are in the same position relative to the transversal and one of the parallel lines. The diagram below has four pairs of corresponding angles: angles 1 and 5; angles 2 and 6; angles 3 and 7; and angles 4 and 8. Corresponding angles formed by parallel lines are congruent.

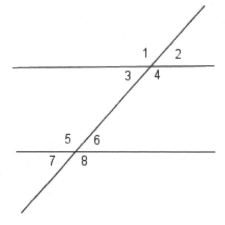

Alternate interior angles and alternate exterior angles

Alternate Interior Angles: When two parallel lines are cut by a transversal, two interior angles that are on opposite sides of the transversal and on opposite parallel lines are congruent opposite interior angles. In the diagram below, there are two pair of alternate interior angles: angles 3 and 6, and angles 4 and 5. Alternate interior angles formed by parallel lines are congruent.

Alternate Exterior Angles: When two parallel lines are cut by a transversal, two exterior angles that are on opposite sides of the transversal and on opposite parallel lines are congruent opposite exterior angles. In the diagram below, there are two pair of alternate exterior angles: angles 1 and 8, and angles 2 and 7. Alternate exterior angles formed by parallel lines are congruent.

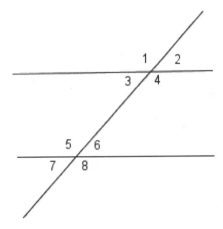

Perpendicular lines and bisectors

Perpendicular lines are lines that intersect at right angles. They are represented by the symbol ⊥. The shortest distance from a line to a point not on the line is a perpendicular segment from the point to the line.

In a plane, the perpendicular bisector of a line segment is a line comprised of the set of all points that are equidistant from the endpoints of the segment. This line always forms a right angle with the segment in the exact middle of the segment. Note that you can only find perpendicular bisectors of segments.

Side, vertex, regular polygon, apothem, and radius

Each straight line segment of a polygon is called a side.

The point at which two sides of a polygon intersect is called the vertex. In a polygon, the number of sides is always equal to the number of vertices.

A polygon with all sides congruent and all angles equal is called a regular polygon.

A line segment from the center of a polygon perpendicular to a side of the polygon is called the apothem. In a regular polygon, the apothem can be used to find the area of the polygon using the formula $A = \frac{1}{2}ap$, where a is the apothem and p is the perimeter.

A line segment from the center of a polygon to a vertex of the polygon is called the radius. The radius of a regular polygon is also the radius of a circle that can be circumscribed about the polygon.

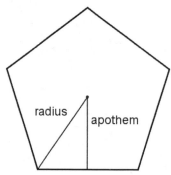

Names for shapes

3 sides: triangle
4 sides: quadrilateral
5 sides: pentagon
6 sides: hexagon
7 sides: heptagon
8 sides: octagon
9 sides: nonagon
10 sides: decagon
12 sides: dodecagon
n sides: n-gon

Sum and measure of the interior angle(s) of a polygon

To find the sum of the interior angles of a polygon, use the formula: sum of interior angles $= (n - 2)180°$, where n is the number of sides in the polygon. This formula works with all polygons, not just regular polygons.

To find the measure of one interior angle of a regular polygon, use the formula $\frac{(n-2)180°}{n}$, where n is the number of sides in the polygon.

Diagonal, convex, concave, polygons

A diagonal is a line segment that joins two non-adjacent vertices of a polygon.

A convex polygon is a polygon whose diagonals all lie within the interior of the polygon.

A concave polygon is a polygon with a least one diagonal that lies outside the polygon. In the diagram below, quadrilateral *ABCD* is concave because diagonal $\overline{AC}$ lies outside the polygon.

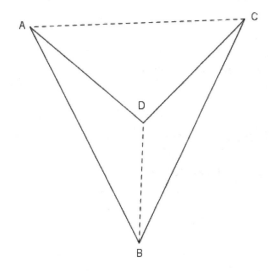

The number of diagonals a polygon has can be found by using the formula: number of diagonals $= \frac{n(n-3)}{2}$, where *n* is the number of sides in the polygon. This formula works for all polygons, not just regular polygons.

Equilateral, isosceles, scalene

An equilateral triangle is a triangle with three congruent sides. An equilateral triangle will also have three congruent angles.

An isosceles triangle is a triangle with two congruent sides. An isosceles triangle will also have two congruent angles opposite the two congruent sides.

A scalene triangle is a triangle with no congruent sides. A scalene triangle will also have three angles of different measures. The angle with the largest measure is opposite the longest side, and the angle with the smallest measure is opposite the shortest side.

Equilateral   Isosceles   Scalene

- 37 -

Acute, right, and obtuse

An acute triangle is a triangle whose three angles are all less than 90º. If two of the angles are equal, the acute triangle is also an isosceles triangle. If the three angles are all equal, the acute triangle is also an equilateral triangle.

A right triangle is a triangle with exactly one angle equal to 90º. All right triangles follow the Pythagorean Theorem. A right triangle can never be acute or obtuse.

An obtuse triangle is a triangle with exactly one angle greater than 90º. The other two angles may or may not be equal. If the two remaining angles are equal, the obtuse triangle is also an isosceles triangle.

The sum of the measures of the interior angles of a triangle is always 180º. Therefore, a triangle can never have more than one angle greater than or equal to 90º.

Triangle Inequality Theorem

The Triangle Inequality Theorem states that the sum of the measures of any two sides of a triangle is always greater than the measure of the third side. If the sum of the measures of two sides were equal to the third side, a triangle would be impossible because the two sides would lie flat across the third side and there would be no vertex. If the sum of the measures of two of the sides was less than the third side, a closed figure would be impossible because the two shortest sides would never meet.

Similar triangles

In any triangle, the angles opposite congruent sides are congruent, and the sides opposite congruent angles are congruent. The largest angle is always opposite the longest side, and the smallest angle is always opposite the shortest side.

The line segment that joins the midpoints of any two sides of a triangle is always parallel to the third side and exactly half the length of the third side.

Similar triangles are triangles whose corresponding angles are equal and whose corresponding sides are proportional. Represented by AA. Similar triangles whose corresponding sides are congruent are also congruent triangles.

Types of congruent triangles

Three sides of one triangle are congruent to the three corresponding sides of the second triangle. Represented as SSS.

Two sides and the included angle (the angle formed by those two sides) of one triangle are congruent to the corresponding two sides and included angle of the second triangle. Represented by SAS.

Two angles and the included side (the side that joins the two angles) of one triangle are congruent to the corresponding two angles and included side of the second triangle. Represented by ASA.

Two angles and a non-included side of one triangle are congruent to the corresponding two angles and non-included side of the second triangle. Represented by AAS.

Note that AAA is not a form for congruent triangles. This would say that the three angles are congruent, but says nothing about the sides. This meets the requirements for similar triangles, but not congruent triangles.

Properties of quadrilaterals

A quadrilateral whose diagonals bisect each other is a parallelogram. A quadrilateral whose opposite sides are parallel (2 pairs of parallel sides) is a parallelogram.

A quadrilateral whose diagonals are perpendicular bisectors of each other is a rhombus. A quadrilateral whose opposite sides (both pairs) are parallel and congruent is a rhombus.

A parallelogram that has a right angle is a rectangle. (Consecutive angles of a parallelogram are supplementary. Therefore if there is one right angle in a parallelogram, there are four right angles in that parallelogram.)

A rhombus with one right angle is a square. Because the rhombus is a special form of a parallelogram, the rules about the angles of a parallelogram also apply to the rhombus.

Center, radius, and diameter

Center: A single point that is equidistant from every point on a circle. (Point O in the diagram below.)

Radius: A line segment that joins the center of the circle and any one point on the circle. All radii of a circle are equal. (Segments OX, OY, and OZ in the diagram below.)

Diameter: A line segment that passes through the center of the circle and has both endpoints on the circle. The length of the diameter is exactly twice the length of the radius. (Segment XZ in the diagram below.)

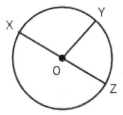

Concentric ,arc and semicircle

Concentric circles are circles that have the same center, but not the same length of radii. A bulls-eye target is an example of concentric circles.

An arc is a portion of a circle. Specifically, an arc is the set of points between and including two points on a circle. An arc does not contain any points inside the circle. When a segment is drawn from the endpoints of an arc to the center of the circle, a sector is formed.

A semicircle is an arc whose endpoints are the endpoints of the diameter of a circle. A semicircle is exactly half of a circle.

Chord, secant, tangent, and point of tangency

Chord: A line segment that has both endpoints on a circle. In the diagram below, $\overline{EB}$ is a chord.

Secant: A line that passes through a circle and contains a chord of that circle. In the diagram below, $\overleftrightarrow{EB}$ is a secant and contains chord $\overline{EB}$.

Tangent: A line in the same plane as a circle that touches the circle in exactly one point. While a line segment can be tangent to a circle as part of a line that is tangent, it is improper to say a tangent can be a line segment by itself that touches the circle in exactly one point. In the diagram below, $\overleftrightarrow{CD}$ is tangent to circle A. Notice that $\overline{FB}$ is not tangent to the circle. $\overline{FB}$ is a line segment that touches the circle in exactly one point, but if the segment were extended, it would touch the circle in a second point.

Point of Tangency: The point at which a tangent touches a circle. In the diagram below, point B is the point of tangency.

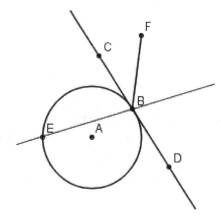

Central angles, major and minor arcs

Central Angle: An angle whose vertex is the center of a circle and whose legs intercept an arc of the circle.

Major Arc: An arc of a circle, having a measure of at least 180º. The measure of the major arc can be found by subtracting the measure of the central angle from 360º.

Minor Arc: An arc of a circle, having a measure less than 180º. The measure of the central angle is equal to the measure of the arc.

Semicircle: An arc having a measure of exactly 180º.

Inscribed angles and intercepted arcs

An inscribed angle is an angle whose vertex lies on a circle and whose legs contain chords of that circle. The portion of the circle intercepted by the legs of the angle is called the intercepted arc. The measure of the intercepted arc is exactly twice the measure of the inscribed angle. In the diagram below, angle ABC is an inscribed angle. arc $AC = 2(m\angle ABC)$

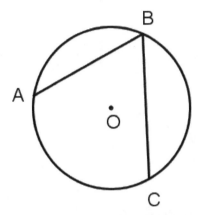

Any angle inscribed in a semicircle is a right angle. The intercepted arc is 180º, making the inscribed angle half that, or 90º. In the diagram below, angle ABC is inscribed in semicircle ABC, making angle B equal to 90º.

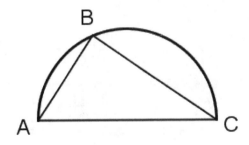

Secants

A secant is a line that intersects a curve in two points. Two secants may intersect inside the circle, on the circle, or outside the circle. When the two secants intersect on the circle, an inscribed angle is formed.

When two secants intersect inside a circle, the measure of each of two vertical angles is equal to half the sum of the two intercepted arcs. In the diagram below, $m\angle AEB = \frac{1}{2}(\text{arc}AB + \text{arc}CD)$ and $m\angle BEC = \frac{1}{2}(\text{arc}BC + \text{arc}AD)$.

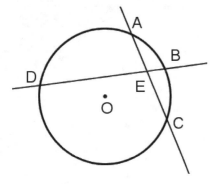

When two secants intersect outside a circle, the measure of the angle formed is equal to half the difference of the two arcs that lie between the two secants. In the diagram below, $m\angle E = \frac{1}{2}(\text{arc}AB - \text{arc}CD)$.

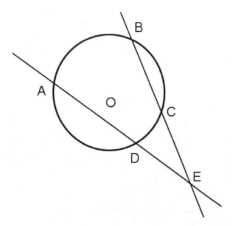

Arc length and sector

The arc length of a circle is the length of a portion of the circumference between two points on the circle. When the arc is defined by two radii forming a central angle, the formula for arc length is $s = r\theta$, where s is the arc length, r is the length of the radius, and θ is the measure of the central angle in radians.

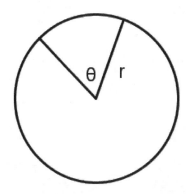

A sector is the portion of a circle formed by two radii and their intercepted arc. While the arc length is exclusively the points that are also on the circumference of the circle, the sector is the entire area bounded by the arc and the two radii.

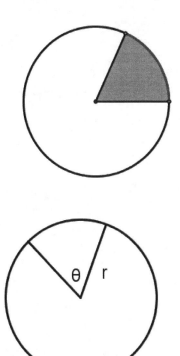

Inscribed and circumscribed

A circle is inscribed in a polygon if each of the sides of the polygon is tangent to the circle. A polygon is inscribed in a circle if each of the vertices of the polygon lies on the circle.

A circle is circumscribed about a polygon if each of the vertices of the polygon lies on the circle. A polygon is circumscribed about the circle if each of the sides of the polygon is tangent to the circle.

If one figure is inscribed in another, then the other figure is circumscribed about the first figure.

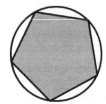

Circle circumscribed about a pentagon
Pentagon inscribed in a circle

Pythagorean Theorem

A right triangle has exactly one right angle. (If a figure has more than one right angle, it must have more than three sides, since the sum of the three angles of a triangle must equal 180º.)

The side opposite the right angle is called the hypotenuse. The other two sides are called the legs.

The Pythagorean Theorem states a unique relationship among the legs and hypotenuse of a right triangle: $a^2 + b^2 = c^2$, where a and b are the lengths of the legs of a right triangle, and c is the length of the hypotenuse. Note that this formula will only work with right triangles. Do not attempt to use it with triangles that are not right triangles.

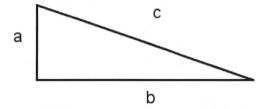

Area and perimeter (triangle)

The area of a triangle is given by the formula $A = \frac{1}{2}bh$, where A is the area of the triangle, b is the length of the base, and h is the height of the triangle perpendicular to the base.

If you know the three sides of a scalene triangle, you can use the formula $A = \sqrt{s(s-a)(s-b)(s-c)}$, where A is the area, s is the semiperimeter $s = \frac{a+b+c}{2}$, and a, b, and c are the lengths of the three sides.

The perimeter of a triangle is given by the formula $P = a + b + c$, where P is the perimeter, and a, b, and c are the lengths of the three sides. In this case, the triangle may be any shape. The variables a, b, and c are not exclusive to right triangles in the perimeter formula.

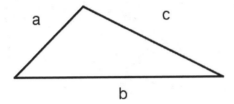

Area and perimeter (square)

The area of a square is found by using the formula $A = s^2$, where A is the area of the square, and s is the length of one side.

The perimeter of a square is found by using the formula $P = 4s$, where P is the perimeter of the square, and s is the length of one side. Because all four sides are equal in a square, it is faster to multiply the length of one side by 4 than to add the same number four times. You could use the formulas for rectangles and get the same answer.

Area and perimeter (rectangle)

The area of a rectangle is found by the formula $A = lw$, where A is the area of the rectangle, l is the length (usually considered to be the longer side) and w is the width (usually considered to be the shorter side). The numbers for l and w are interchangeable.

The perimeter of a rectangle is found by the formula $P = 2l + 2w$ or $P = 2(l + w)$, where P is the perimeter of the rectangle, l is the length, and w is the width. It may be easier to add the length and width first and then double the result, as in the second formula.

Area and perimeter (parallelogram)

The area of a parallelogram is found by the formula $A = bh$, where A is the area, b is the length of the base, and h is the height. Note that the base and height correspond to the length and width in a rectangle, so this formula would apply to rectangles as well.

The perimeter of a parallelogram is found by the formula $P = 2a + 2b$ or $P = 2(a + b)$, where P is the perimeter, and a and b are the lengths of the two sides.

Do not confuse the height of a parallelogram with the length of the second side. The two are only the same measure in the case of a rectangle.

Area and perimeter (trapezoid)

The area of a trapezoid is found by the formula $A = \frac{1}{2}h(b_1 + b_2)$, where A is the area, h is the height (segment joining and perpendicular to the parallel bases), and b_1 and b_2 are the two parallel sides (bases). Do not use one of the other two sides as the height unless that side is also perpendicular to the parallel bases.

The perimeter of a trapezoid is found by the formula $P = a + b_1 + c + b_2$, where P is the perimeter, and a, b_1, c, and b_2 are the four sides of the trapezoid. Notice that the height does not appear in this formula.

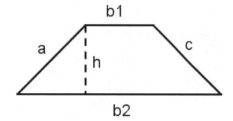

Area, circumference, and diameter (circle)

The area of a circle is found by the formula $A = \pi r^2$, where A is the area and r is the length of the radius. If the diameter of the circle is given, remember to divide it in half to get the length of the radius before proceeding.

The circumference of a circle is found by the formula $C = 2\pi r$, where C is the circumference and r is the radius. Again, remember to convert the diameter if you are given that measure rather than the radius.

To find the diameter when you are given the radius, double the length of the radius.

Area and arc length (sector of a circle)

The area of a sector of a circle is found by the formula $= \frac{\theta r^2}{2}$, where A is the area, θ is the measure of the central angle in radians, and r is the radius. To find the area when the central angle is in degrees, use the formula $= \frac{\theta \pi r^2}{360}$, where θ is the measure of the central angle in degrees and r is the radius.

The arc length of a sector of a circle is found by the formula: arc length $= r\theta$, where r is the radius and θ is the measure of the central angle in radians. To find the arc length when the central angle is given in degrees, use the formula: arc length $= \frac{\theta(2\pi r)}{360}$, where θ is the measure of the central angle in degrees and r is the radius.

Lateral surface area and volume (sphere)

The lateral surface area is the area around the outside of the sphere. The lateral surface area is given by the formula $A = 4\pi r^2$, where r is the radius. The answer is generally given in terms of pi. A sphere does not have separate formulas for lateral surface area and total surface area as other solid figures do. Often, a problem may ask for the surface area of a sphere. Use the above formula for all problems involving the surface area of a sphere.

The volume is given by the formula $V = \frac{4}{3}\pi r^3$, where r is the radius.

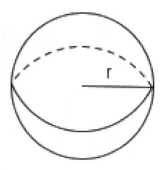

Volume and total surface area (right prism)

The volume of a right prism is found by the formula $V = Bh$, where V is the volume, B is the area of the base, and h is the height (perpendicular distance between the bases).

The total surface area is the area of the entire outside surface of a solid. The total surface area of a right prism is found by the formula $TA = 2B + $ (sum of the areas of the sides), where TA is the total surface area and B is the area of one base. To use this formula, you must remember the formulas for the planar figures.

If the problem asks for the lateral surface area (the area around the sides, not including the bases), use the formula $LA = $ sum of the areas of the sides. Again, you will need to remember the formulas for the various planar figures.

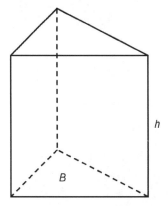

Volume and total surface area (rectangular prism)

The volume of a rectangular prism is found by the formula $V = lwh$, where V is the volume, l is the length, w is the width, and h is the height.

Total surface area is the area of the entire outside surface of the solid. The total surface area of a rectangular prism is found by the formula $TA = 2lw + 2lh + 2wh$ or $TA = 2(lw + lh + wh)$, where TA is the total surface area, l is the length, w is the width, and h is the height.

If the problem asks for lateral surface area, find the total area of the sides, but not the bases. Use the formula $LA = 2lh + 2wh$ or $LA = 2(lh + wh)$, where l is the length, w is the width, and h is the height.

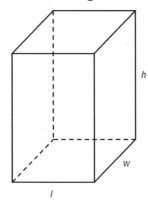

Volume and total surface area (cube)

The volume of a cube is found by the formula $V = s^3$, where V is the volume and s is the length of a side. This is the same as the formula for the volume of a rectangular prism, except the length, width, and height are all equal.

The total surface area of a cube is found by the formula $TA = 6s^2$, where TA is the total surface area and s is the length of a side. You could use the formula for the total surface area of a rectangular prism, but if you remember that all six sides of a cube are equal, this formula is much faster.

Volume, lateral surface area, and total surface area (right circular cylinder)

The volume of a right circular cylinder is found by the formula $V = \pi r^2 h$, where V is the volume, r is the radius, and h is the height.

The lateral surface area is the surface area without the bases. The formula is $LA = 2\pi rh$, where LA is the lateral surface area, r is the radius, and h is the height. Remember that if you unroll a cylinder, the piece around the middle is a rectangle. The length of a side of the rectangle is equal to the circumference of the circular base, or $2\pi r$. Substitute this formula for the length, and substitute the height of the cylinder for the width in the formula for the area of a rectangle. The total surface area of a cylinder is the lateral surface area plus the area of the two bases. The bases of a cylinder are circles, making the formula for the total

- 48 -

surface area of a right circular cylinder $TA = 2\pi rh + 2\pi r^2$, where TA is the total area, r is the radius, and h is the height.

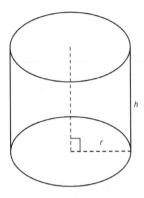

Pyramid volume

The volume of a pyramid is found by the formula $V = \frac{1}{3}Bh$, where V is the volume, B is the area of the base, and h is the height (segment from the vertex perpendicular to the base). Notice this formula is the same as $\frac{1}{3}$ the volume of a right prism. In this formula, B represents the *area* of the base, not the length or width of the base. The base can be different shapes, so you must remember the various formulas for the areas of plane figures. In determining the height of the pyramid, use the perpendicular distance from the vertex to the base, not the slant height of one of the sides.

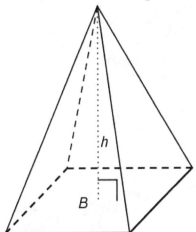

Volume, lateral surface area, and total surface area (right circular cone)

The volume of a right circular cone is found by the formula $V = \frac{1}{3}\pi r^2 h$, where V is the volume, r is the radius, and h is the height. Notice this is the same as $\frac{1}{3}$ the volume of a right circular cylinder.

The lateral surface area of a right circular cone is found by the formula $LA = \pi r\sqrt{r^2 + h^2}$ or $LA = \pi rs$, where LA is the lateral surface area, r is the radius, h is the height, and s is the slant height (distance from the vertex to the edge of the circular base). $s = \sqrt{r^2 + h^2}$

- 49 -

The total surface area of a right circular cone is the same as the lateral surface area plus the area of the circular base. The formula for total surface area is $TA = \pi r \sqrt{r^2 + h^2} + \pi r^2$ or $TA = \pi rs + \pi r^2$, where TA is the total surface area, r is the radius, h is the height, and s is the slant height.

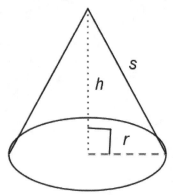

Area and perimeter (equilateral triangle)

The area of an equilateral triangle is found by the formula $A = \frac{\sqrt{3}}{4}s^2$, where A is the area and s is the length of a side. You could use the $30° - 60° - 90°$ ratios to find the height of the triangle and then use the standard triangle area formula, but this is faster.

The perimeter of an equilateral triangle is found by the formula $P = 3s$, where P is the perimeter and s is the length of a side.

If you know the length of the apothem (distance from the center of the triangle perpendicular to the base) and the length of a side, you can use the formula $A = \frac{1}{2}ap$, where a is the length of the apothem and p is the perimeter.

Area and perimeter (isosceles triangle)

The area of an isosceles triangle is found by the formula, $A = \frac{1}{2}b\sqrt{a^2 - \frac{b^2}{4}}$, where A is the area, b is the base (the unique side), and a is the length of one of the two congruent sides.

If you do not remember this formula, you can use the Pythagorean Theorem to find the height so you can use the standard formula for the area of a triangle.

The perimeter of an isosceles triangle is found by the formula$A = 2a + b$, where P is the perimeter, a is the length of one of the congruent sides, and b is the base (the unique side).

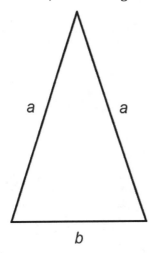

Preimage, image, translation, reflection, rotation, and dilation

Preimage: The original unchanged image in its original position.

Image: A unique set of points

Translation: A case where a geometric image is slid, usually horizontally or vertically. The resulting image is congruent to the original image, but has been moved in a straight line.

Reflection: A case where a geometric image is flipped across a line of reflection. The resulting image is congruent to and a mirror image of the original image.

Rotation: A case where a geometric image is rotated around the center of rotation to a new position. The new image is congruent to the original image, but has been turned to a new position.

Dilation: A case where a geometric image has been expanded or contracted by a scale factor. The resulting image is similar to the original image, but not congruent.

Projection of a point and segment on a line

The projection of a point on a line is the point at which a perpendicular line drawn from the given point to the given line intersects the line. This is also the shortest distance from the given point to the line.

The projection of a segment on a line is a segment whose endpoints are the points formed when perpendicular lines are drawn from the endpoints of the given segment to the given line. This is similar to the length a diagonal line *appears* to be when viewed from above.

Ellipse that is taller than it is wide

An ellipse is the set of all points in a plane, whose total distance from two fixed points called the foci (singular: focus) is constant, and whose center is the midpoint between the foci.

The standard equation of an ellipse that is taller than it is wide is $\frac{(y-k)^2}{a^2} + \frac{(x-h)^2}{b^2} = 1$, where a and b are coefficients. The center is the point (h, k) and the foci are the points $(h, k + c)$ and $(h, k - c)$, where $c^2 = a^2 - b^2$ and $a^2 > b^2$.

The major axis has length $2a$, and the minor axis has length $2b$.

Eccentricity (e) is a measure of how elongated an ellipse is, and is the ratio of the distance between the foci to the length of the major axis. Eccentricity will have a value between 0 and 1. The closer to 1 the eccentricity is, the closer the ellipse is to being a circle. The formula for eccentricity is $= \frac{c}{a}$.

Ellipse that is wider than it is tall

The standard equation of an ellipse that is wider than it is tall is $\frac{(x-h)^2}{a^2} + \frac{(y-k)^2}{b^2} = 1$, where a and b are coefficients. The center is the point (h, k) and the foci are the points $(h + c, k)$ and $(h - c, k)$, where $c^2 = a^2 - b^2$ and $a^2 > b^2$.

The major axis has length $2a$, and the minor axis has length $2b$.

Eccentricity (e) is a measure of how elongated an ellipse is, and is the ratio of the distance between the foci to the length of the major axis. Eccentricity will have a value between 0 and 1. The closer to 1 the eccentricity is, the closer the ellipse is to being a circle. The formula for eccentricity is $= \frac{c}{a}$.

Geometric description of parabola

Parabola: The set of all points in a plane that are equidistant from a fixed line, called the directrix, and a fixed point not on the line, called the focus.

Axis: The line perpendicular to the directrix that passes through the focus.

For parabolas that open up or down, the standard equation is $(x - h)^2 = 4c(y - k)$, where h, c, and k are coefficients. If c is positive, the parabola opens up. If c is negative, the parabola opens down. The vertex is the point (h, k). The directrix is the line having the equation $y = -c + k$, and the focus is the point $(h, c + k)$.

For parabolas that open left or right, the standard equation is $(y - k)^2 = 4c(x - h)$, where k, c, and h are coefficients. If c is positive, the parabola opens to the right. If c is negative, the parabola opens to the left. The vertex is the point (h, k). The directrix is the line having the equation $x = -c + h$, and the focus is the point $(c + h, k)$.

Geometric description of horizontal hyperbola

A hyperbola is the set of all points in a plane, whose distance from two fixed points, called foci, has a constant difference.

The standard equation of a horizontal hyperbola is $\frac{(x-h)^2}{a^2} - \frac{(y-k)^2}{b^2} = 1$, where a, b, h, and k are real numbers. The center is the point (h, k), the vertices are the points $(h + a, k)$ and $(h - a, k)$, and the foci are the points that every point on one of the parabolic curves is equidistant from and are found using the formulas $(h + c, k)$ and $(h - c, k)$, where $c^2 = a^2 + b^2$. The asymptotes are two lines the graph of the hyperbola approaches but never reaches, and are given by the equations $y = \left(\frac{b}{a}\right)(x - h) + k$ and $y = -\left(\frac{b}{a}\right)(x - h) + k$.

Geometric description of vertical hyperbola

A vertical hyperbola is formed when a plane makes a vertical cut through two cones that are stacked vertex-to-vertex.

The standard equation of a vertical hyperbola is $\frac{(y-k)^2}{a^2} - \frac{(x-h)^2}{b^2} = 1$, where a, b, k, and h are real numbers. The center is the point (h, k), the vertices are the points $(h, k + a)$ and $(h, k - a)$, and the foci are the points that every point on one of the parabolic curves is equidistant from and are found using the formulas $(h, k + c)$ and $(h, k - c)$, where $c^2 = a^2 + b^2$. The asymptotes are two lines the graph of the hyperbola approaches but never reach, and are given by the equations $y = \left(\frac{a}{b}\right)(x - h) + k$ and $y = -\left(\frac{a}{b}\right)(x - h) + k$.

Trigonometric ratios of right triangles

$$\sin A = \frac{\text{opposite side}}{\text{hypotenuse}} = \frac{a}{c}$$

$$\cos A = \frac{\text{adjacent side}}{\text{hypotenuse}} = \frac{b}{c}$$

$$\tan A = \frac{\text{opposite side}}{\text{adjacent side}} = \frac{a}{b}$$

$$\csc A = \frac{\text{hypotenuse}}{\text{opposite side}} = \frac{c}{a}$$

$$\sec A = \frac{\text{hypotenuse}}{\text{adjacent side}} = \frac{c}{b}$$

$$\cot A = \frac{\text{adjacent side}}{\text{opposite side}} = \frac{b}{a}$$

In the diagram below, angle C is the right angle, and side c is the hypotenuse. Side a is the side adjacent to angle B and side b is the side adjacent to angle A. These formulas will work for any acute angle in a right triangle. They will NOT work for any triangle that is not a right triangle. Also, they will not work for the right angle in a right triangle, since there is not a distinct adjacent side to differentiate from the hypotenuse.

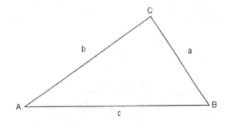

Measurement equivalents

<u>1 yard in feet and inches</u>
1 yard = 3 feet
1 yard = 36 inches

<u>1 mile in feet and yards</u>
1 mile = 5280 feet
1 mile = 1760 yards

<u>1 acre in square feet</u>
1 acre = 43,560 square feet

<u>1 quart in pints and cups</u>
1 quart = 2 pints
1 quart = 4 cups

<u>1 gallon in quarts, pints, and cups</u>
1 gallon = 4 quarts
1 gallon = 8 pints
1 gallon = 16 cups

<u>1 pound in ounces</u>
1 pound = 16 ounces

Do not assume that because something weighs one pound that its volume is one pint. Ounces of weight are not equivalent to fluid ounces, which measure volume.

<u>1 ton in pounds</u>
1 ton = 2000 pounds

In the United States, the word "ton" by itself refers to a short ton or a net ton. Do not confuse this with a long ton (also called a gross ton) or a metric ton (also spelled *tonne*), which have different measurement equivalents.

Fluid measurements

<u>1 cup in fluid ounces</u>
1 cup = 8 fluid ounces

Note: This does NOT mean that one cup of something is the same as a half pound. Fluid ounces are measures of volume and have no correspondence with measures of weight.

<u>1 pint in cups and fluid ounces</u>
1 pint = 2 cups
1 pint = 16 ounces

Again, the phrase, "A pint's a pound the world round," does not apply. A pint of something does not necessarily weigh one pound, since one fluid ounce is not the same as one ounce in weight. The expression is valid only for helping you remember the number 16, since most people can remember there are 16 ounces in a pound.

Metric measurements

<u>1 liter in milliliters and cubic centimeters</u>
1 liter = 1000 milliliters
1 liter = 1000 cubic centimeters

Do not confuse *cubic centimeters* with *centiliters*. 1 liter = 1000 cubic centi*meters*, but 1 liter = 100 centi*liters*.

<u>1 meter in millimeters and centimeters</u>
1 meter = 1000 millimeters
1 meter = 100 centimeters

<u>1 gram in milligrams</u>
1 gram = 1000 milligrams

<u>1 kilogram in grams</u>
1 kilogram = 1000 grams

Kilo, centi, and milli

Kilo-: one thousand (1 *kilo*gram is one thousand grams.)
Centi-: one hundredth (1 *centi*meter is one hundredth of a meter.)
Milli-: one thousandth (1 *milli*liter is one thousandth of a liter.)

Converting unit measurements

When going from a larger unit to a smaller unit, multiply the numerical value of the known amount by the equivalent amount. When going from a smaller unit to a larger unit, divide the numerical value of the known amount by the equivalent amount. Also, you can set up conversion fractions where one fraction is the conversion fact, with the unit of the unknown amount in the numerator and the unit of the known value in the denominator. The second fraction has the known value from the problem in the numerator, and the unknown in the denominator. Multiply the two fractions to get the converted measurement.

Precision and accuracy

Precision: How reliable and repeatable a measurement is. The more consistent the data is with repeated testing, the more precise it is. For example, hitting a target consistently in the same spot, which may or may not be the center of the target, is precision.

Accuracy: How close the data is to the correct data. For example, hitting a target consistently in the center area of the target, whether or not the hits are all in the same spot, is accuracy.

Note that it is possible for data to be precise without being accurate. If a scale is off balance, the data will be precise, but will not be accurate. For data to have precision and accuracy, it must be repeatable and correct.

Approximate and maximum possible error

Approximate Error: The amount of error in a physical measurement. Approximate error is often reported as the measurement, followed by the ± symbol and the amount of the approximate error.

Maximum Possible Error: Half the magnitude of the smallest unit used in the measurement. For example, if the unit of measurement is 1 centimeter, the maximum possible error is $\frac{1}{2}$ cm, written as ± 0.5 cm following the measurement. It is important to apply significant figures in reporting maximum possible error. Do not make the answer appear more accurate than the least accurate of your measurements.

Probability and Statistics

Sample space and outcome

The total number of all possible results of a random test or experiment is called a sample space, or sometimes a universal sample space. The sample space, represented by one of the variables S, Ω, or U (for universal sample space) has individual elements called outcomes. Other terms for outcome that may be used interchangeably include elementary outcome, simple event, or sample point. The number of outcomes in a given sample space could be infinite or finite, and some tests may yield multiple unique sample sets. For example, tests conducted by drawing playing cards from a standard deck would have one sample space of the card values, another sample space of the card suits, and a third sample space of suit-denomination combinations. Note that on this test, all sample spaces are considered finite.

Event

An event, represented by the variable E, is a portion of a sample space. It may be one outcome or a group of outcomes from the same sample space. If an event occurs, then the test or experiment will generate an outcome that satisfies the requirement of that event. For example, given a standard deck of 52 playing cards as the sample space, and defining the event as the collection of face cards, then the event will occur if the card drawn is a J, Q, or K. If any other card is drawn, the event is said to have not occurred.

Probability measure and probability

For every sample space, each possible outcome has a specific likelihood, or probability, that it will occur. The probability measure, also called the distribution, is a function that assigns a real number probability, from zero to one, to each outcome. For a probability measure to be accurate, every outcome must have a real number probability measure that is greater than or equal to zero and less than or equal to one. Also, the probability measure of the sample space must equal one, and the probability measure of the union of multiple outcomes must equal the sum of the individual probability measures.

Probability of an event

Probabilities of events are expressed as real numbers from zero to one. They give a numerical value to the chance that a particular event will occur. The probability of an event occurring is the sum of the probabilities of the individual elements of that event. For example, in a standard deck of 52 playing cards as the sample space and the collection of face cards as the event, the probability of drawing a specific face card is $\frac{1}{52} = 0.019$, but the probability of drawing any one of the twelve face cards is $12(0.019) = 0.228$. Note that rounding of numbers can generate different results. If you multiplied 12 by the fraction $\frac{1}{52}$ before converting to a decimal, you would get the answer $\frac{12}{52} = 0.231$. If, when taking the exam, you get an answer that is not a choice, try the other method.

Likelihood of outcomes

The likelihood of a outcome occurring, or the probability of an outcome occurring, is given by the formula $P(E) = \frac{\text{Number of possible events}}{\text{Total number of possible outcomes in the sample space}}$ where $P(E)$ is the probability of an event E occurring, and each outcome is just as likely to occur as any other outcome. If each outcome has the same probability of occurring as every other possible outcome, the outcomes are said to be equally likely to occur. The total number of possible outcomes in the event must be less than or equal to the total number of possible outcomes in the sample space. If the two are equal, then the event is certain to occur and the probability is 1. If the number of outcomes that satisfy the event is zero, then the event is impossible and the probability is 0.

Simple sample space outcome

For a simple sample space, possible outcomes may be determined by using a tree diagram or an organized chart. In either case, you can easily draw or list out the possible outcomes. For example, to determine all the possible ways three objects can be ordered, you can draw a tree diagram:

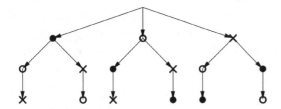

You can also make a chart to list all the possibilities:

First object	Second object	Third object
●	X	O
●	O	X
O	●	X
O	X	●
X	●	O
X	O	●

Either way, you can easily see there are six possible ways the three objects can be ordered.

Less straightforward sample space outcome

When the test on a given sample space does not lend itself to a tree diagram or organized chart, you can use other methods, such as the multiplication principle, permutations, or combinations, to determine the total number of possible outcomes. Each of these may also be used for simple sample spaces as well, although tree diagrams or charts may be faster in those situations.

The multiplication rule states that the probability of two outcomes occurring simultaneously is the product of their individual probabilities.

Permutations are outcomes in which each element must occur in a specific order. Combinations are outcomes in which the elements may be arranged in any order.

Permutations and combinations

A permutation is an arrangement of a specific number of a set of objects in a specific order. No unique combination of elements from the set may be rearranged and used a second time. To find the number of possible outcomes from a group of items, use the formula $_nP_r = \frac{n!}{(n-r)!}$, where n is the total number of items in the set, r is the number of distinct objects taken together from the set, and $_nP_r$ is the number of permutations of those objects taken together.

Combinations are similar to permutations, except there are no restrictions regarding the order of the elements. While ABC is considered a different permutation than BCA, ABC and BCA are considered the same combination. To calculate the number of unique combinations possible from a given set, use the formula $_nC_r = \binom{n}{r} = \frac{n!}{r!(n-r)!}$, where n is the total number of items in the set, r is the number of distinct objects taken together from the set, and $_nC_r$ is the number of combinations of those objects.

Note that a combination lock should be called a permutation lock because the order of the numbers is important when unlocking the lock.

Random variable and probability distribution

In probability, the random variable is not really a variable, but rather a function that generates a variable with a real number value that is determined purely by chance and assigned to each possible outcome of a sample space. Once the values of the random variable have been determined, a probability distribution is set up. The probability distribution can be a chart, graph, formula, or table that gives the individual probabilities of all the values of the random variable. It described the range of possibilities for the random variable, and gives the probability of the random variable falling somewhere within that range.

Event complement

The complement of an event is the opposite of the probability of an event occurring. Represented by the symbol $\bar{A}$, it is the probability that event A does not happen. When you know the probability of event A occurring, you can use the formula $(\bar{A}) = 1 - P(A)$, where $P(\bar{A})$ is the probability of event A not occurring, and $P(A)$ is the probability of event A occurring, to find the complement of the event.

Compound events are events that combine two or more events into a single desired outcome. (Think of it like compound words combining two words into a single new word.) For compound events, the notation $P(A \text{ or } B)$ means the probability that event A occurs, or event B occurs, or events A and B occur at the same time during the same test of an experiment.

Addition Rule for probability

The addition rule for probability is used for finding the probability of a compound event. Use the formula $P(A \text{ or } B) = P(A) + P(B) - P(A \text{ and } B \text{ occurring at the same time})$, where $P(A)$ is the probability of the event A occurring exclusively, $P(B)$ is the probability of event B occurring exclusively, and $P(A \text{ and } B \text{ occurring at the same time})$ is the probability of both events occurring to find the probability of a compound event. The probability of both events occurring at the same time must be subtracted to eliminate any overlap in the first two probabilities.

Multiplication Rule for probability

The multiplication rule can be used to find the probability of two independent events occurring using the formula $P(A \text{ and } B) = P(A) \, P(B)$, where $P(A \text{ and } B)$ is the probability of two independent events occurring, $P(A)$ is the probability of the first event occurring, and $P(B)$ is the probability of the second event occurring.

The multiplication rule can also be used to find the probability of two dependent events occurring using the formula $P(A \text{ and } B) = P(A) \cdot P(B|A)$, where $P(A \text{ and } B)$ is the probability of two dependent events occurring, $P(A)$ is the probability of the first event occurring, and $P(B|A)$ is the probability of the second event occurring after the first event has already occurred.

Before using the multiplication rule, you MUST first determine whether the two events are dependent or independent.

Mutually exclusive, independent, and dependent

If two events have no outcomes in common, they are said to be mutually exclusive. For example, in a standard deck of 52 playing cards, the event of all card suits is mutually exclusive to the event of all card values. If two events have no bearing on each other so that one event occurring has no influence on the probability of another event occurring, the two events are said to be independent. For example, rolling a standard six-sided die multiple times does not change that probability that a particular number will be rolled from one roll to the next. If the outcome of one event does affect the probability of the second event, the two events are said to be dependent. For example, if cards are drawn from a deck, the probability of drawing an ace after an ace has been drawn is different than the probability of drawing an ace if no ace (or no other card, for that matter) has been drawn.

Conditional probability

Conditional probability is the probability of a dependent event occurring once the original event has already occurred. Given event A and dependent event B, the probability of event B occurring when event A has already occurred is represented by the notation $P(A|B)$. To find the probability of event B occurring, take into account the fact that event A has already occurred and adjust the total number of possible outcomes. For example, suppose you have ten balls numbered 1–10 and you want ball number 7 to be pulled in two pulls. On the first pull, the probability of getting the 7 is $\frac{1}{10}$ because there is one ball with a 7 on it and 10 balls to choose from. Assuming the first pull did not yield a 7, the probability of pulling a 7 on the second pull is now $\frac{1}{9}$ because there are only 9 balls remaining for the second pull.

Probability that at least one of something will occur

Use a combination of the multiplication rule and the rule of complements to find the probability that at least one outcome of the element will occur. This given by the general formula $P(\text{at least one event occurring}) = 1 - P(\text{no outcomes occurring})$. For example, to find the probability that at least one even number will show when a pair of dice is rolled, find the probability that two odd numbers will be rolled (no even numbers) and subtract from one. You can always use a tree diagram or make a chart to list the possible outcomes when the sample space is small, such as in the dice-rolling example, but in most cases it will be much faster to use the multiplication and complement formulas.

Odds in favor

In probability, the odds in favor of an event are the number of times the event will occur compared to the number of times the event will not occur. To calculate the odds in favor of an event, use the formula $\frac{P(A)}{1-P(A)}$, where $P(A)$ is the probability that the event will occur. Many times, odds in favor is given as a ratio in the form $\frac{a}{b}$ or $a:b$, where a is the probability of the event occurring and b is the complement of the event, the probability of the event not occurring. If the odds in favor are given as 2:5, that means that you can expect the event to occur two times for every 5 times that it does not occur. In other words, the probability that the event will occur is $\frac{2}{2+5} = \frac{2}{7}$.

Odds against

In probability, the odds against an event are the number of times the event will not occur compared to the number of times the event will occur. To calculate the odds against an event, use the formula $\frac{1-P(A)}{P(A)}$, where $P(A)$ is the probability that the event will occur. Many times, odds against is given as a ratio in the form $\frac{b}{a}$ or $b:a$, where b is the probability the event will not occur (the complement of the event) and a is the probability the event will occur. If the odds against an event are given as 3:1, that means that you can expect the event to not occur 3 times for every one time it does occur. In other words, 3 out of every 4 trials will fail.

Expected value

Expected value is a method of determining expected outcome in a random situation. It is really a sum of the weighted probabilities of the possible outcomes. Multiply the probability of an event occurring by the weight assigned to that probability (such as the amount of money won or lost). A practical application of the expected value is to determine whether a game of chance is really fair. If the sum of the weighted probabilities is greater than or equal to zero, the game is generally considered fair because the player has a fair chance to win, or at least to break even. If the expected value is less than one, then players lose more than they win. For example, a lottery drawing allows the player to choose any three-digit number, 000–999. The probability of choosing the winning number is 1:1000. If it costs $1 to play, and a winning number receives \$500, the expected value is $\left(-\$1 \cdot \frac{999}{1,000}\right) +$ $\left(\$500 \cdot \frac{1}{1,000}\right) = -0.499$ or $-\$0.50$. You can expect to lose on average 50 cents for every dollar you spend.

Empirical probability

Empirical probability is based on conducting numerous repeated experiments and observations rather than by applying pre-defined formulas to determine the probability of an event occurring. To find the empirical probability of an event, conduct repeated trials (repetitions of the same experiment) and record your results. The empirical probability of an event occurring is the number of times the event occurred in the experiment divided by the total number of trials you conducted to get the number of events. Notice that the total number of trials is used, not the number of unsuccessful trials. A practical application of empirical probability is the insurance industry. There are no set functions that define life span, health, or safety. Insurance companies look at factors from hundreds of thousands of individuals to find patterns that they then use to set the formulas for insurance premiums.

Objective and subjective probability

Objective probability is based on mathematical formulas and documented evidence. Examples of objective probability include raffles or lottery drawings where there is a pre-determined number of possible outcomes and a predetermined number of outcomes that correspond to an event. Other cases of objective probability include probabilities of rolling dice, flipping coins, or drawing cards. Most gambling is based on objective probability.

Subjective probability is based on personal or professional feelings and judgments. Often, there is a lot of guesswork following extensive research. Areas where subjective probability is applicable include sales trends and business expenses. Attractions set admission prices based on subjective probabilities of attendance based on varying admission rates in an effort to maximize their profit.

Charts and tables

Charts and tables are ways of organizing information in separate rows and columns that are each labeled to identify and explain the data contained in them. Some charts and tables are organized horizontally, with row lengths giving the details about the labeled information. Other charts and tables are organized vertically, with column heights giving the details about the labeled information.

Frequency tables show how frequently each unique value appears in the set. A relative frequency table is one that shows the proportions of each unique value compared to the entire set. Relative frequencies are given as percents; however, the total percent for a relative frequency table will not necessarily equal 100 percent due to rounding.

Pictograph

A pictograph is a graph, generally in the horizontal orientation, that uses pictures or symbols to represent the data. Each pictograph must have a key that defines the picture or symbol and gives the quantity each picture or symbol represents. Pictures or symbols on a pictograph are not always shown as whole elements. In this case, the fraction of the picture or symbol shown represents the same fraction of the quantity a whole picture or symbol stands for. For example, a row with $3\frac{1}{2}$ ears of corn, where each ear of corn represents 100 stalks of corn in a field, would equal $3\frac{1}{2} \cdot 100 = 350$ stalks of corn in the field.

Circle graphs

Circle graphs, also known as pie charts, provide a visual depiction of the relationship of each type of data compared to the whole set of data. The circle graph is divided into sections by drawing radii to create central angles whose percentage of the circle is equal to the individual data's percentage of the whole set. Each 1% of data is equal to 3.6º in the circle graph. Therefore, data represented by a 90º section of the circle graph makes up 25% of the whole. When complete, a circle graph often looks like a pie cut into uneven wedges.

Line graph

Line graphs have one or more lines of varying styles (solid or broken) to show the different values for a set of data. The individual data are represented as ordered pairs, much like on a Cartesian plane. In this case, the *x*- and *y*-axes are defined in terms of their units, such as dollars or time. The individual plotted points are joined by line segments to show whether the value of the data is increasing (line slanting upward), decreasing (line slanting downward) or staying the same (horizontal line). Multiple sets of data can be graphed on the same line graph to give an easy visual comparison. An example of this would be graphing achievement test scores for different groups of students over the same time period to see which group had the greatest increase or decrease in performance from year-to-year.

Line plot

A line plot, also known as a dot plot, has plotted points that are NOT connected by line segments. In this graph, the horizontal axis lists the different possible values for the data, and the vertical axis lists the number of times the individual value occurs. A single dot is graphed for each value to show the number of times it occurs. This graph is more closely related to a bar graph than a line graph. Do not connect the dots in a line plot or it will misrepresent the data.

Stem and leaf plot

A stem and leaf plot is useful for depicting groups of data that fall into a range of values. Each piece of data is separated into two parts: the first, or left, part is called the stem; the second, or right, part is called the leaf. Each stem is listed in a column from smallest to largest. Each leaf that has the common stem is listed in that stem's row from smallest to largest. For example, in a set of two-digit numbers, the digit in the tens place is the stem, and the digit in the ones place is the leaf. With a stem and leaf plot, you can easily see which subset of numbers (10s, 20s, 30s, etc.) is the largest. This information is also readily available by looking at a histogram, but a stem and leaf plot also allows you to look closer and see exactly which values fall in that range.

- 63 -

Bar graph

A bar graph is one of the few graphs that can be drawn correctly in two different configurations – both horizontally and vertically. A bar graph is similar to a line plot in the way the data is organized on the graph. Both axes must have their categories defined for the graph to be useful. Rather than placing a single dot to mark the point of the data's value, a bar, or thick line, is drawn from zero to the exact value of the data, whether it is a number, percentage, or other numerical value. Longer bar lengths correspond to greater data values. To read a bar graph, read the labels for the axes to determine the units being reported. Then look where the bars end in relation to the scale given on the corresponding axis and read the number.

Histogram

At first glance, a histogram looks like a vertical bar graph. The difference is that a bar graph has a separate bar for each piece of data and a histogram has one continuous bar for each *range* of data. For example, a histogram may have one bar for the range 0–9, one bar for 10–19, etc. While a bar graph has numerical values on one axis, a histogram has numerical values on both axes. Each range is of equal size, and they are ordered left to right from lowest to highest. The height of each column on a histogram represents the number of data values within that range. Like a stem and leaf plot, a histogram makes it easy to glance at the graph and quickly determine which range has the greatest quantity of values.

Scatter plot

Bivariate data is simply data from two different variables. (The prefix *bi-* means *two.*) In a scatter plot, each value in the set of data is plotted on a grid similar to a Cartesian plane, where each axis represents one of the two variables. By looking at the pattern formed by the points on the grid, you can easily determine whether or not there is a relationship between the two variables, and what that relationship is, if it exists. The variables may be directly proportionate, inversely proportionate, or show no proportion at all. It will also be easy to determine if the data is linear, and if so, to find an equation to relate the two variables.

Central tendency

The measure of central tendency is a statistical value that gives a general tendency for the center of a group of data. There are several different ways of describing the measure of central tendency. Each one has a unique way it is calculated, and each one gives a slightly different perspective on the data set. Whenever you give a measure of central tendency, always make sure the units are the same. If the data has different units, such as hours, minutes, and seconds, convert all the data to the same unit, and use the same unit in the measure of central tendency. If no units are given in the data, do not give units for the measure of central tendency.

Statistical mean

The statistical mean of a group of data is the same as the arithmetic average of that group. To find the mean of a set of data, first convert each value to the same units, if necessary. Then find the sum of all the values, and count the total number of data values, making sure you take into consideration each individual value. If a value appears more than once, count it more than once. Divide the sum of the values by the total number of values and apply the units, if any. Note that the mean does not have to be one of the data values in the set, and may not divide evenly.

$$\text{mean} = \frac{\text{sum of the data values}}{\text{quantity of data values}}$$

Central tendency

While the mean is relatively easy to calculate and averages are understood by most people, the mean can be very misleading if used as the sole measure of central tendency. If the data set has outliers (data values that are unusually high or unusually low compared to the rest of the data values), the mean can be very distorted, especially if the data set has a small number of values. If unusually high values are countered with unusually low values, the mean is not affected as much. For example, if five of the twenty students in a class get a 100 on a test, but the other 15 students have an average of 60 on the same test, the class average would appear as 70. Whenever the mean is skewed by outliers, it is always a good idea to include the median as an alternate measure of central tendency.

The big disadvantage of using the median as a measure of central tendency is that is relies solely on a value's relative size as compared to the other values in the set. When the individual values in a set of data are evenly dispersed, the median can be an accurate tool. However, if there is a group of rather large values or a group of rather small values that are not offset by a different group of values, the information that can be inferred from the median may not be accurate.

The main disadvantage of the mode is that the values of the other data in the set have no bearing on the mode. The mode may be the largest value, the smallest value, or a value anywhere in between in the set. The mode only tells which value or values, if any, occurred the most number of times. It does not give any suggestions about the remaining values in the set.

Statistical median

The statistical median value is the value in the middle of the set of data. To find the median, list all data values in order from smallest to largest or from largest to smallest. Any value that is repeated in the set must be listed the same number of times. If there are an odd number of data values, the median is the value in the middle of the list. If there is an even number of data values, the median is the arithmetic mean of the two middle values.

Statistical mode

The statistical mode is the data value that occurs the most number of times in the data set. It is possible to have exactly one mode, more than one mode, or no mode. To find the mode of a set of data, arrange the data like you do to find the median (all values in order, listing all multiples of data values). Count the number of times each value appears in the data set. If all values appear an equal number of times, there is no mode. If one value appears more than any other value, that value is the mode. If two or more values appear the same number of times, but there are other values that appear fewer times and no values that appear more times, all of those values are the modes.

Measure of dispersion

The measure of dispersion is a single value that helps to "interpret" the measure of central tendency by providing more information about how the data values in the set are distributed about the measure of central tendency. The measure of dispersion helps to eliminate or reduce the disadvantages of using the mean, median, or mode as a single measure of central tendency, and give a more accurate picture of the data set as a whole. To have a measure of dispersion, you must know or calculate the range, standard deviation, or variance of the data set.

Range

The range of a set of data is the difference between the greatest and lowest values of the data in the set. To calculate the range, you must first make sure the units for all data values are the same, and then identify the highest and lowest values. Using the values with the same units, use the formula range = highest value – lowest value. If there are multiple data values that are equal for the highest or lowest, just use one of the values in the formula. Write the answer with the same units as the data values you used to do the calculations.

Standard deviation

Standard deviation is a measure of dispersion that compares all the data values in the set to the mean of the set to give a more accurate picture. To find the standard deviation of a population, use the formula $= \sqrt{\frac{\sum_{i=1}^{n}(x_i-\bar{x})^2}{n}}$, where σ is the standard deviation of a population, x represents the individual values in the data set, $\bar{x}$ is the mean of the data values in the set, and n is the number of data values in the set. The higher the value of the standard deviation is, the greater the variance of the data values from the mean.

Variance

The variance of a population, or just variance, is the square of the standard deviation of that population. While the mean of a set of data gives the average of the set and gives information about where a specific data value lies in relation to the average, the variance of the population gives information about the degree to which the data values are spread out and tell you how close an individual value is to the average compared to the other values. The units associated with variance are the same as the units of the data values. If there are different units used among the data values, you must first convert all the values to the same unit.

Percentiles and quartiles

Percentiles and quartiles are other methods of describing data within a set. Percentiles tell what percentage of the data in the set fall below a specific point. For example, achievement test scores are often given in percentiles. A score at the 80th percentile is one which is equal to or higher than 80 percent of the scores in the set. In other words, 80 percent of the scores were lower than that score.

Quartiles are percentile groups that make up quarter sections of the data set. The first quartile is the 25th percentile. The second quartile is the 50th percentile. This is also the median of the data set. The third quartile is the 75th percentile.

Five number summary

The 5-number summary of a set of data gives a very informative picture of the set. The five numbers in the summary include the minimum value, maximum value, and the three quartiles. This information gives the reader the range and median of the set, as well as an indication of how the data is spread about the median.

A box-and-whiskers plot is a graphical representation of the 5-number summary. To draw a box-and-whiskers plot, plot the points of the 5-number summary on a number line. Draw a box whose ends are through the points for the first and third quartiles. Draw a vertical line in the box through the median to divide the box in half. Draw a line segment from the first quartile point to the minimum value, and from the third quartile point to the maximum value.

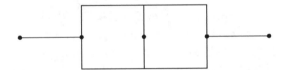

Skewness

Skewness is a way to describe the symmetry or asymmetry of the distribution of values in a data set. If the distribution of values is symmetrical, there is no skew. In general the closer the mean of a data set is to the median of the data set, the less skew there is. Generally, if the mean is to the right of the median, the data set is positively skewed, or right-skewed, and if the mean is to the left of the median, the data set is negatively skewed, or left-skewed. However, this rule of thumb is not infallible. When the data values are graphed on a curve, a set with no skew will be a perfect bell curve. To estimate skew, use the formula

$$\text{skew} = \frac{\sqrt{n(n-1)}}{n-2}\left(\frac{\frac{1}{n}\sum_{i=1}^{n}(x_i-\bar{x})^3}{\left(\frac{1}{n}\sum_{i=1}^{n}(x_i-\bar{x})^2\right)^{\frac{3}{2}}}\right)$$ where n is the number of values is the set, x_i is the ith

value in the set, and $\bar{x}$ is the mean of the set.

Simple regression

In statistics, simple regression is using an equation to represent a relation between independent and dependent variables in the data. The independent variable is also referred to as the explanatory variable or the predictor, and is generally represented by the variable x in the equation. The dependent variable, usually represented by the variable y, is also referred to as the response variable. The equation may be any type of function – linear, quadratic, exponential, etc. The best way to handle this task is to use the regression feature of your graphing calculator. This will easily give you the curve of best fit and provide you with the coefficients and other information you need to derive an equation.

Scatter plots

Scatter plots are useful in determining the type of function represented by the data and finding the simple regression. Linear scatter plots may be positive or negative. Nonlinear scatter plots are generally exponential or quadratic. You must be able to identify the following types of scatter plots on the test:

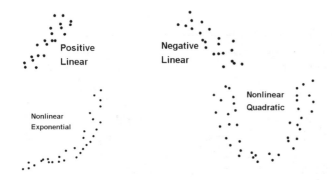

Line of best fit, regression coefficients, residuals, and least-squares regression line

In a scatter plot, the line of best fit is the line that best shows the trends of the data. The line of best fit is given by the equation $\hat{y} = ax + b$, where a and b are the regression coefficients. The regression coefficient a is also the slope of the line of best fit, and b is also the y-coordinate of the point at which the line of best fit crosses the x-axis. Not every point on the scatter plot will be on the line of best fit. The differences between the y-values of the points in the scatter plot and the corresponding y-values according to the equation of the line of best fit are the residuals. The line of best fit is also called the least-squares regression line because it is also the line that has the lowest sum of the squares of the residuals.

Correlation coefficient

The correlation coefficient is a numerical value that indicates how strong the relationship is between the two variables of a linear regression equation. A correlation coefficient of –1 is a perfect negative correlation. A correlation coefficient of +1 is a perfect positive correlation. Correlation coefficients close to –1 or +1 are very strong correlations. A correlation coefficient equal to zero indicates there is no correlation between the two variables. This test is a good indicator of whether or not the equation for the line of best fit is accurate. The formula for the correlation coefficient is $r = \dfrac{\sum_{i=1}^{n}(x_i-\bar{x})(y_i-\bar{y})}{\sqrt{\sum_{i=1}^{n}(x_i-\bar{x})^2}\sqrt{\sum_{i=1}^{n}(y_i-\bar{y})^2}}$ where r is the correlation coefficient, n is the number of data values in the set, (x_i, y_i) is a point in the set, and $\bar{x}$ and $\bar{y}$ are the means.

68-95-99.7 rule

The 69–95–99.7 rule describes how a normal distribution of data should appear when compared to the mean. This is also a description of a normal bell curve. According to this rule, 68 percent of the data values in a normally distributed set should fall within one standard deviation of the mean (34 percent above and 34 percent below the mean), 95 percent of the data values should fall within two standard deviations of the mean (47.5 percent above and 47.5 percent below the mean), and 99.7 percent of the data values should fall within three standard deviations of the mean, again, equally distributed on either side of the mean. This means that only 0.3 percent of all data values should fall more than three standard deviations from the mean.

Z-scores

A z-score is an indication of how many standard deviations a given value falls from the mean. To calculate a z-score, use the formula $= \frac{x - \mu}{\sigma}$, where x is the data value, μ is the mean of the data set, and σ is the standard deviation of the population. If the z-score is positive, the data value lies above the mean. If the z-score is negative, the data value falls below the mean. These scores are useful in interpreting data such as standardized test scores, where every piece of data in the set has been counted, rather than just a small random sample. In cases where standard deviations are calculated from a random sample of the set, the z-scores will not be as accurate.

Population and parameter

In statistics, the population is the entire set of data to be included in the study, rather than just a random sample. For example, a study to determine how well students in the area schools perform on a standardized test would have a population of all the students enrolled in those schools, although a study may include a random sample of students from each school. A parameter is a numerical value that gives information about the population, such as the mean, median, mode, or standard deviation. Remember that the symbol for the mean of a population is μ and the symbol for the standard deviation of a population is σ.

Sample and statistic

A sample is a portion of the entire population. A statistic is a numerical value that gives information about the sample, such as mean, median, mode, or standard deviation. Keep in mind that the symbols for mean and standard deviation are different when they are referring to a sample rather than the entire population. For a sample, the symbol for mean is $\bar{x}$ and the symbol for standard deviation is s. The mean and standard deviation of a sample may or may not be accurate when compared to the mean and standard deviation of the population. However, if the sample is random and large enough, an accurate enough value can be obtained. Samples are generally used when the population is too large to justify including every element.

Inferential statistics and sampling distribution

Inferential statistics is the branch of statistics that uses samples to make predictions about an entire population. This type of statistics is often seen in political polls, where a sample of the population is questioned about a particular topic or politician to gain an understanding about the attitudes of the entire population of the country. Often, exit polls are conducted on election days using this method. Inferential statistics can have a large margin of error if you do not have a valid sample.

The statistical values calculated from the various samples of the same size make up the sampling distribution. For example, if several samples of identical size are randomly selected from a large population and then the mean of each sample is calculated, the values of the means would be a sampling distribution.

Sampling distribution of the mean

Represented by the symbol $\bar{x}$, the sampling distribution of the mean has three important characteristics. First, the mean of the sampling distribution of $\bar{x}$ equals the mean of the sampled population. The sampled population includes all of the samples in the distribution combined. Second, assuming the standard deviation is positive, the standard deviation of the sampling distribution of $\bar{x}$ equals the standard deviation of the sampled population divided by the square root of the sample size. Finally, as the sample size gets larger and closer to the actual population number, the sampling distribution of $\bar{x}$ gets closer to a normal distribution.

Central Limit Theorem

According to the central limit theorem, no matter what the original distribution of a sample is, the distribution of the means tends to get closer and closer to a normal distribution as the sample size gets larger and larger. In other words, if you have a large population that does not represent a normal distribution, and then take random samples of two elements from that population, the means of the groups of two will form a more normal distribution. Increase the sample size to three elements for each calculation of the mean, and the distribution gets more normal than with a sample size of two. This pattern will continue to form a more normal distribution of the means as the sample size increases.

Survey studies

A survey study is a method of gathering information from a small group in an attempt to gain enough information to make accurate general assumptions about the population. Once a survey study is completed, the results are then put into a summary report.

Survey studies are generally in the format of surveys, interviews, or questionnaires as part of an effort to find opinions of a particular group or to find facts about a group.

It is important to note that the findings from a survey study are only as accurate as the sample chosen from the population. Inappropriate samples, such as ones that are too small for the population size, or ones that are not chosen purely at random, will not yield accurate results for the population. Generalizations concerning the population cannot be made in these cases.

Correlational studies

Correlational studies seek to determine how much one variable is affected by changes in a second variable. For example, correlational studies may look for a relationship between the amount of time a student spends studying for a test and the grade that student earned on the test, between student scores on college admissions tests and student grades in college, or between employment status and degrees earned.

It is important to note that correlational studies cannot show a cause and effect, but rather can show only that two variables are or are not potentially related.

Experimental studies

Experimental studies take correlational studies one step farther, in that they attempt to prove or disprove a cause-and-effect relationship. These studies are performed by conducting a series of experiments to test the hypothesis. For a study to be scientifically accurate, it must have both an experimental group that receives the specified treatment and a control group that does not get the treatment. This is the type of study pharmaceutical companies do as part of drug trials for new medications. Experimental studies are only valid when proper scientific method has been followed. In other words, the experiment must be well-planned and executed without bias in the testing process. All subjects must be selected at random, and the process of determining which subject is in which of the two groups must also be completely random.

Observational studies

Observational studies are the opposite of experimental studies. In observational studies, the tester cannot change or in any way control all of the variables in the test. For example, a study to determine which gender does better in math classes in school is strictly observational. You cannot change a person's gender, and you cannot change the subject being studied. The big downfall of the observational study is that you have no way of proving a cause-and-effect relationship because you cannot control outside influences. Events outside of school can influence a student's performance in school, and observational studies would not take that into consideration

Type of samples

A sample is a piece of the entire population that is selected for a particular study in an effort to gain knowledge or information about the entire population. For most studies, a random sample is necessary to produce valid results. Random samples should not have any particular influence to cause someone to select that element over another. The goal is for the random sample to be a representative sample, or a sample whose characteristics give an accurate picture of the characteristics of the entire population. To accomplish this, you must make sure you have a proper sample size, or an appropriate number of elements in the sample.

Bias and extraneous variables

In statistical studies, try to avoid bias at all costs. Bias is an error that causes the study to favor one set of results over another. For example, if a survey to determine how the country views the president's job performance only speaks to registered voters in the president's party, the results will be skewed because a disproportionately large number of responders would tend to show approval, while a disproportionately large number of people in the opposite party would tend to express disapproval.

Extraneous variables are outside influences that can affect the outcome of a study. They are not always avoidable, but could trigger bias in the result.

Frequency curves

The five general shapes of frequency curves are symmetrical, U-shaped, skewed, J-shaped, and multimodal. Symmetrical curves are also known as bell curves or normal curves. Values equidistant from the median have equal frequencies. U-shaped curves have two maxima – one at each end. Skewed curves have the maximum point off-center. Curves that are negative skewed, or left skewed, have the maximum on the right side of the graph so there is longer tail and lower slope on the left side. The opposite is true for curves that are positive skewed, or right skewed. J-shaped curves have a maximum at one end and a minimum at the other end. Multimodal curves have multiple maxima. If the curve has exactly two maxima, it is called a bimodal curve.

Fundamental Counting Principle

The Fundamental Counting Principle deals specifically with situations in which the order that something happens affects the outcome. Specifically, the Fundamental Counting Principle states that if one event can have x possible different outcomes, and after the first outcome has been established the event can then have y possible outcomes, then there are $x \cdot y$ possible different ways the outcomes can happen in that order. For example, if two dice are rolled, one at a time, there are 6 possible outcomes for the first die, and 6 possible outcomes for the second die, for a total of $6 \cdot 6 = 36$ total possible outcomes. Also, suppose you have a bag containing one each of a penny, nickel, dime, quarter, and half dollar. There are 5 different possible outcomes the first time you pull a coin. Without replacing the first coin, there are 4 different possible outcomes for the second coin. This makes $5 \cdot 4 = 20$ different possible outcomes for the first two coins drawn when the order the coins are drawn makes a difference.

Addition Principle

The Addition Principle addresses situations in which two different tasks are completed at separate times with separate outcomes. The Addition Principle states that if one event can have x possible different outcomes, and a second unrelated event can have y possible different outcomes, and none of the outcomes are common to both events, then the total number of possible outcomes for the two separate events occurring at two separate times is $x + y$. If the two events can occur at the same time and some of the outcomes are common to both events, the total number of possible outcomes for the two events is $x + y -$ the number of outcomes common to both events.

Permutation

For each set of data, the individual elements may be arranged in different groups containing different numbers of elements arranged in different orders. For example, given the set of integers from one to three, inclusive, the elements of the set are 1, 2, and 3. They may be arranged as follows: 1, 2, 3, 12, 21, 13, 31, 23, 32, 123, 132, 231, 213, 312, and 321. These ordered sequences of elements from the given set of data are called permutations. It is important to note that in permutations, the order of the elements in the sequence is important. The sequence 123 is not the same as the sequence 213. Also, no element in the given set may be used more times as an element in a permutation than it appears as an element in the original set. For example, 223 is not a permutation in the above example because the number 2 only appears one time in the given set.

Factorial of a number

The factorial of a positive integer is represented by the ! sign. The factorial of a number is the product of the number and all positive integers less than the number. For example, 3! (read "3 factorial") means $3 \cdot 2 \cdot 1 = 6$. The exception to the rule is the case of zero factorial. In this case, $0! = 1$. This makes sense if you consider the pattern of factorials:

$$4! = 4 \cdot 3 \cdot 2 \cdot 1 = 24;$$
$$3! = 3 \cdot 2 \cdot 1 = \frac{4!}{4} = 6;$$
$$2! = 2 \cdot 1 = \frac{3!}{3} = 2;$$
$$1! = \frac{2!}{2} = 1;$$
$$0! = \frac{1!}{1} = 1$$

Number of permutations

The number of possible permutations of n items from a set of n items is $n!$, or $n(n-1)(n-2)(n-3) \ldots (3)(2)(1)$. To find the number of permutations of r items from a set of n items, use the formula $_nP_r = \frac{n!}{(n-r)!}$. When using this formula, each element of r must be unique. Also, this assumes that different arrangements of the same set of elements yields different outcomes. For example, 123 is not the same as 321; order is important! If the set contains duplicates of one or more elements, the formula changes slightly to accommodate the duplicates. Use the formula $= \frac{n!}{n_1!n_2!\ldots n_k!}$, where P is the number of permutations, n is the total number of elements in the set, and n_1, n_2, and n_3 are the number of duplicates of an individual element.

To find the total number of possible permutations of a set of unique items, you must apply the permutation formulas multiple times. For example, to find the total number of possible permutations of the set 1, 2, 3, first apply the formula $P = n!$ as follows: $P = n! = 3! = 6$. This gives the number of permutations of the three elements when all three elements are used. To find the number of permutations when two of the three elements are used, use the formula
$_nP_r = \frac{n!}{(n-r)!}$, where n is 3 and r is 2.

$$_nP_r = \frac{n!}{(n-r)!} \Rightarrow {_3P_2} = \frac{3!}{(3-2)!} = \frac{6}{1} = 6$$

To find the number of permutations when one element is used, use the formula
$_nP_r = \frac{n!}{(n-r)!}$, where n is 3 and r is 1.

- 73 -

$$_nP_r = \frac{n!}{(n-r)!} \Rightarrow {}_3P_1 = \frac{3!}{(3-1)!} = \frac{3!}{2!} = \frac{6}{2} = 3$$

Find the sum of the three formulas: $6 + 6 + 3 = 15$ total possible permutations.

Combinations

For each set of data, the individual elements may be arranged in different groups containing different numbers of elements arranged in different orders. For example, given the set of integers from one to three, inclusive, the elements of the set are 1, 2, and 3. They may be arranged as follows: 1, 2, 3, 12, 21, 13, 31, 23, 32, 123, 132, 231, 213, 312, and 321. Some of the arrangements contain the exact same elements as other arrangements and must be discarded to avoid duplicates. This leaves 1, 2, 3, 12, 13, 23, and 123. These sequences of unique combinations of elements from the given set of data are called combinations. No element in the given set may be used more times as an element in a combination than it appears as an element in the original set. For example, 223 is not a combination in the above example because the number 2 only appears one time in the given set.

Difference between permutations and combinations

The biggest difference between permutations and combinations is the ordering of the sequences. In permutations, different sequences of the same group of elements create different permutations. In combinations, different sequences of the same group of elements create the same combination. It is easy to get the two terms confused, especially since the terms are misused in the English language. For example, combination locks do not require a combination, but a permutation. If you enter the correct numbers in the wrong order, you have entered a correct combination, but an incorrect permutation, and the lock will not open.

Number of combinations

In a set containing n elements, the number of combinations of r items from the set can be found using the formula $_nC_r = \frac{n!}{r!(n-r)!}a$. Notice the similarity to the formula for permutations. In effect, you are dividing the number of permutations by $r!$ to get the number of combinations, and the formula may be written $_nC_r = \frac{nP_r}{r!}$. When finding the number of combinations, it is important to remember that the elements in the set must be unique, that is, there must not be any duplicate items, and that no item is used more than once in any given sequence.

Recursive definition relative to a Fibonacci sequence

Whenever one element of a sequence is defined in terms of a previous element or elements of the sequence, the sequence has a recursive definition. For example, given the recursive definition $a_1 = 0; a_2 = 1; a_n = a_{n-1} + a_{(n-2)}$ for all $n \geq 2$, you get the sequence 0, 1, 1, 2, 3, 5, 8, ... This particular sequence is known as the Fibonacci sequence, and is defined as the numbers zero and one, and a continuing sequence of numbers, with each number in the sequence equal to the sum of the two previous numbers. It is important to note that the Fibonacci sequence can also be defined as the first two terms being equal to one, with the

- 74 -

remaining terms equal to the sum of the previous two terms. Both definitions are considered correct in mathematics. Make sure you know which definition you are working with when dealing with Fibonacci numbers.

Recursive sequence closed form expression

Sometimes one term of a sequence with a recursive definition can be found without knowing the previous terms of the sequence. This case is known as a closed-form expression for a recursive definition. In this case, an alternate formula will apply to the sequence to generate the same sequence of numbers. However, not all sequences based on recursive definitions will have a closed-form expression. Some sequences will require the use of the recursive definition. For example, the Fibonacci sequence has a closed-form expression given by the formula $(n) = \frac{\phi^n - \left(\frac{-1}{\phi}\right)^n}{\sqrt{5}}$, where $f(n)$ is the nth term in the sequence, and φ is the golden ratio, which is equal to $\frac{1+\sqrt{5}}{2}$. In this case, $f(1) = 1$, so you know which definition of the Fibonacci sequence you have.

Cartesian product

A Cartesian product is the product of two sets of data, X and Y, such that all elements x are a member of set X, and all elements y are a member of set Y. The product of the two sets, $X \times Y$ is the set of all ordered pairs (x, y). For example, given a standard deck of 52 playing cards, there are four possible suits (hearts, diamonds, clubs, and spades) and thirteen possible card values (the numbers 2 through 10, ace, jack, queen, and king). If the card suits are set X and the card values are set Y, then there are $4 \times 13 = 52$ possible different (x, y) combinations, as seen in the 52 cards of a standard deck.

Binary relation

A binary relation, also referred to as a relation, dyadic relation, or 2-place relation, is a subset of a Cartesian product. It shows the relation between one set of objects and a second set of object, or between one set of objects and itself. The prefix *bi-* means *two*, so there are always two sets involved – either two different sets, or the same set used twice. The ordered pairs of the Cartesian product are used to indicate a binary relation. Relations are possible for situations involving more than two sets, but those are not called binary relations.

Types of relations

The five types of relations are reflexive, symmetric, transitive, antisymmetric, and equivalence. A reflexive relation has $x\Re x$ (x related to x) for all values of x in the set. A symmetric relation has $x\Re y \Rightarrow y\Re x$ for all values of x and y in the set. A transitive relation has $(x\Re y \text{ and } y\Re z) \Rightarrow x\Re z$ for all values of x, y, and z in the set. An antisymmetric relation has $(x\Re y \text{ and } y\Re x) \Rightarrow x = y$ for all values of x and y in the set. A relation that is reflexive, symmetric, and transitive is called an equivalence relation. These definitions will be provided in the test booklet.

Sequence

Any function with the set of all natural numbers as the domain is also called a sequence. An element of a sequence is denoted by the symbol a_n, which represents the nth element of sequence a. Sequences may be arithmetic or geometric, and may be defined by a recursive definition, closed-form expression or both. Both arithmetic and geometric sequences have recursive definitions based on the first term of the sequence. Both arithmetic and geometric sequences also have formulas to find the sum of the first n terms in the sequence, assuming you know what the first term is. The sum of all the terms in a sequence is called a series.

Arithmetic sequence

An arithmetic sequence, or arithmetic progression, is a special kind of sequence in which each term has a specific quantity, called the common difference, that is added to the previous term. The common difference may be positive or negative. The general form of an arithmetic sequence containing n terms is $a_1, a_1 + d, a_1 + 2d, \dots, a_1 + (n-1)d$, where d is the common difference. The formula for the general term of an arithmetic sequence is $a_n = a_1 + (n-1)d$, where a_n is the term you are looking for and d is the common difference. To find the sum of the first n terms of an arithmetic sequence, use the formula $s_n = \frac{n}{2}(a_1 + a_n)$.

Geometric sequence

A geometric sequence, or geometric progression, is a special kind of sequence in which each term has a specific quantity, called the common ratio, multiplied by the previous term. The common ratio may be positive or negative. The general form of a geometric sequence containing n terms is $a_1, a_1 r, a_1 r^2, \dots, a_1 r^{n-1}$, where r is the common ratio. The formula for the general term of a geometric sequence is $a_n = a_1 r^{n-1}$, where a_n is the term you are looking for and r is the common ratio. To find the sum of the first n terms of a geometric sequence, use the formula $s_n = \frac{a_1(1-r^n)}{1-r}$.

Discrete math

Among mathematicians, there is not an agreed-upon definition of discrete math. What is agreed upon is the fact that discrete math deals with processes that use a finite, or countable, number of elements. In discrete math, the elements will be discontinuous, as this branch of mathematics does not involve the continuity that processes of calculus do. Generally, discrete math uses countable sets of rational numbers, although they do not use the set of all real numbers, as that would then make the math continuous and put it in the category of algebra or calculus. Discrete math has numerous applications in the fields of computer science and business.

Difference equation

Some systems or equations depend on the past values to determine future values. One example of this is the difference equation, which generates values recursively. The difference equation can generate recursive values in the form of a sequence of numbers, such as the Fibonacci sequence, where each element in the sequence depends on the value of previous elements in the sequence. The general form of a difference equation is $(n+1) - f(n) = g(n)$, where n is a positive integer. Another form of the difference

- 76 -

equation is a discrete dynamic system that has a specific equation to follow based on the input of a value to determine the output value. The third type of difference equation is an iterated map, which generates complex orbits of values.

First and second difference

The first difference of a difference equation is used to explain growth rate or decline within a sequence. The equation for the first difference is $\Delta a_n = a_{n+1} - a_n$, where Δa_n is the change, such as the growth or decline of a sequence. If Δa_n is positive, the elements of the sequence are increasing in value. If Δa_n is negative, the elements of the sequence are decreasing in value. If the value of Δa_n is constant, then the rate of increase or decrease is constant and the elements form a linear relationship.

The second difference of a difference equation is $\Delta a_{n+1} = \Delta a_n$. When this value is constant, the elements form a quadratic relationship.

Vertex-edge graph

A vertex-edge graph is useful for solving problems involving schedules, relationships, networks, or paths among a set number of objects. The number of objects may be large, but it will never be infinite. The vertices or points on the graph represent the objects and are referred to as *nodes*. The nodes are joined by line segments called *edges* or links that show the specific paths that connect the various elements represented by the nodes. The number of nodes does not have to equal the number of edges. There may be more or less, depending on the number of allowable paths.

An endpoint on a vertex-edge graph is a vertex on exactly one edge. In the case of a vertex that is an endpoint, the edge that the vertex is on is incident with the vertex. Two edges are considered to be adjacent if they share a vertex. Two vertices are considered to be adjacent if they share an edge.

Loop and degree sum formula

In a vertex-edge graph, a loop is an edge that has the same vertex as both endpoints. To calculate the degree of a vertex in a vertex-edge graph, count the number of edges that are incident with the vertex, counting loops twice since they meet the vertex at both ends. The degree sum formula states that the sum of the degrees of all vertices on a vertex-edge graph is always equal to twice the number of edges on the graph. Thus, the sum of the degrees will never be odd, even if there are an odd number of vertices.

Paths

In a vertex-edge graph, a path is a given sequence of vertices that follows one or more edges to get from vertex to vertex. There is no jumping over spaces to get from one vertex to the next, although doubling back over an edge already traveled is allowed. A simple path is a path that does not repeat an edge in traveling from beginning to end. Think of the vertex-edge graph as a map, with the vertices as cities on the map, and the edges as roads between the cities. To get from one city to another, you must drive on the roads. A simple path allows you to complete your trip without driving on the same road twice.

Circuits

In a vertex-edge graph, a circuit is a path that has the same starting and stopping point. Picturing the vertex-edge graph as a map with cities and roads, a circuit is like leaving home on vacation and then returning home after you have visited your intended destinations. You may go in one direction and then turn around, or you may go in a circle. A simple circuit on the graph completes the circuit without repeating an edge. This is like going on vacation without driving on the same road twice.

Euler and Hamiltonian path

On a vertex-edge graph, any path that uses each edge exactly one time is called an Euler path. One simple way to rule out the possibility of an Euler path is to calculate the degree of each vertex. If more than two vertices have an odd degree, an Euler path is impossible. A path that uses each vertex exactly one time is called a Hamiltonian path.

If every pair of vertices is joined by an edge, the vertex-edge graph is said to be connected. If the vertex-edge graph has no simple circuits in it, then the graph is said to be a tree.

Mathematical Processes and Perspectives

Proofs

A proof serves to show the deductive or inductive process that relates the steps leading from a hypothesis to a conclusion. A proof may be direct ($p \rightarrow q$), meaning that a conclusion is shown to be true, given a hypothesis. There are also proofs by contradiction ($p \wedge \sim q$), whereby the hypothesis is assumed to be true, and the negation of the conclusion is assumed to be true. (In other words, the statement is assumed to be false.) Proofs by contraposition ($\sim q \rightarrow \sim p$) show that the negation of the conclusion leads to the negation of the hypothesis. (In other words, the negation of the conclusion is assumed to be true, and it must be shown that the negation of the hypothesis is also true.) A mathematical induction proof seeks to show that $P(1)$ is true and that $P(k + 1)$ is true, given that $P(k)$ is true. Direct proofs, proofs by contradiction, and proofs by contraposition use deductive methods, while a mathematical induction proof uses an inductive method.

Direct proofs are those that assume a statement to be true. The purpose of such a proof is to show that the conclusion is true, given that the hypothesis is true. A sample of a direct proof is shown below:

Prove "If m divides a and m divides b, then m divides a + b."

Proof:
- Assume m divides a and m divides b.
- Thus, a equals the product of m and some integer factor, p, by the definition of division, and b equals the product of m and some integer factor, q, by the definition of division. According to substitution, a + b may be rewritten as $(m \cdot p) + (m \cdot q)$. Factoring out the m gives $m(p + q)$. Since m divides p + q, and p + q is an integer, according to the closure property, we have shown that m divides a + b, by the definition of division.

Indirect proofs (or proofs by contradiction) are those that assume a statement to be false. The purpose of such a proof is to show that a hypothesis is false, given the negation of the conclusion, indicating that the conclusion must be true. A sample of an indirect proof is shown below:

Prove "If 3x + 7 is odd, then x is even."

Proof:
- Assume 3x + 7 is odd and x is odd.
- According to the definition of odd, x = 2a + 1, where a is an element of the integers.
- Thus, by substitution, 3x + 7 = 3(2a + 1) + 7, which simplifies as 6a + 3 + 7, or 6a + 10, which may be rewritten as 2(3a + 5). Any even integer may be written as the product of 2 and some integer, k. Thus, we have shown the hypothesis to be false, meaning that the conditional statement must be true.

A proof by contraposition is one written in the form, $\sim q \rightarrow \sim p$. In other words, a proof by contraposition seeks to show that the negation of q will yield the negation of p. A sample of a proof by contraposition is shown below:

Prove "If 5x + 7 is even, then x is odd."

Proof:
- Assume that if x is even, then 5x + 7 is odd.
- Assume x is even.
- Thus, by the definition of an even integer, x = 2a.

By substitution, 5x + 7 may be rewritten as 5(2a) + 7, which simplifies as 10a + 7. This expression cannot be written as the product of 2 and some factor, k. Thus, 5x + 7 is odd, by definition of an odd integer. So, when 5x + 7 is even, x is odd, according to contraposition.

A proof by contradiction is one written in the form, $p \wedge \sim q$. In other words, a proof by contradiction seeks to show the negation of q will result in a false hypothesis, indicating that the conclusion of the statement, as written, must be true. In other words, the conditional statement of $p \rightarrow q$ is true.

A proof by mathematical induction must first show that $P(1)$ is true. Once that is shown, such a proof must show that $P(k + 1)$ is true when $P(k)$ is true. A sample proof by induction is shown below:

Prove "If n is a natural number, then $2 + 4 + 6 + 8 + \cdots + 2n = n(n + 1)$."

Show that $P(1)$ is true.
$2(1) = 1(1 + 1)$.

Assume P(k) is true.
$2 + 4 + 6 + 8 + \cdots + 2k = k(k + 1)$

We want to show that $2 + 4 + 6 + 8 + \cdots + 2(k + 1) = (k + 1)((k + 1) + 1)$.
$2 + 4 + 6 + 8 + \cdots + 2(k + 1) = k(k + 1) + 2(k + 1)$.
$2 + 4 + 6 + 8 + \cdots + 2(k + 1) = (k + 1)(k + 2)$.

$P(k + 1)$ is true. Thus, according to mathematical induction, $2 + 4 + 6 + 8 + \cdots + 2n = n(n + 1)$.

Problem

Use any proof type to prove the following: "The sum of the natural numbers is equal to n^2."

Proof by induction:

Show that $P(1)$ is true.
$1 = 1^2$.

Assume $P(k)$ is true.
$1 + 3 + 5 + 7 + \cdots + 2k + 1 = k^2$.

We want to show that $1 + 3 + 5 + 7 + \cdots + 2(k+1) + 1 = (k+1)^2$.
$2 + 4 + 6 + 8 + \cdots + 2(k+1) = k^2 + 2(k+1)$.
$2 + 4 + 6 + 8 + \cdots + 2(k+1) = k^2 + 2k + 2$.

P(k+1) is true. Thus, according to mathematical induction,
$1 + 3 + 5 + 7 + \cdots + 2n + 1 = n^2$.

Premise and argument

A premise is a statement that precedes a conclusion, in an argument. It is the proposition, or assumption, of an argument.

An argument will have two or more premises.

Example:

If it is hot, then I will go swimming. (Premise)
It is hot. (Premise)

_____

Therefore, I will go swimming. (Conclusion)

Truth table to validate the Rule of Detachment

The Rule of Detachment states that given the premises, $p \rightarrow q$ and p, the valid conclusion is q.

In other words, for every case where $(p \rightarrow q) \wedge p$ is true, q will also be true. The truth table below illustrates this fact:

p	q	$p \rightarrow q$	$(p \rightarrow q) \bigwedge p$
T	T	T	T
T	F	F	F
F	T	T	F
F	F	T	F

Notice the first cell under $(p \rightarrow q) \wedge p$ is true, while the first cell under q is also true. Thus, for every case where $(p \rightarrow q) \wedge p$ was true, q was also true.

Truth table to validate the Chain Rule

The Chain Rule states that given the premises, $p \to q$ and $q \to r$, the valid conclusion is $p \to r$.

In other words, for every case where $(p \to q) \wedge (q \to r)$ is true, $p \to r$ will also be true. The truth table below illustrates this fact:

p	q	r	$p \to q$	$q \to r$	$(p \to q) \bigwedge (q \to r)$	$p \to r$
T	T	T	T	T	T	T
T	T	F	T	F	F	F
T	F	T	F	T	F	T
T	F	F	F	T	F	F
F	T	T	T	T	T	T
F	T	F	T	F	F	T
F	F	T	T	T	T	T
F	F	F	T	T	T	T

Notice that for every case where $(p \to q) \wedge (q \to r)$ was true, $p \to r$ was also true.

Consider the premises below:
- If I hike a mountain, I will not eat a sandwich.
- If I do not eat a sandwich, I will drink some water.
- I will not drink some water.

Write a valid conclusive statement. Explain how you arrived at your answer. Be specific in your explanation.

Valid conclusive statement: I will not hike a mountain.

Application of the chain rule and rule of contraposition give the valid conclusion of $\sim p$. According to the chain rule, given $p \to \sim q$ and $\sim q \to r$, then $p \to r$. According to the rule of contraposition, $p \to r$ and $\sim r$ yields $\sim p$. On a truth table, for every place where $(p \to r) \wedge \sim r$ is true, $\sim p$ is also true. Thus, this is a valid conclusive statement.

Inductive reasoning

Inductive reasoning is a method used to make a conjecture, based on patterns and observations. The conclusion of an inductive argument may be true or false.

Mathematical Example:
- A cube has 6 faces, 8 vertices, and 12 edges. A square pyramid has 5 faces, 5 vertices, and 8 edges. A triangular prism has 5 faces, 6 vertices, and 9 edges. Thus, the sum of the numbers of faces and vertices, minus the number of edges, will always equal 2, for any solid.

Non-Mathematical Example:
- Almost all summer days in Tucson are hot. It is a summer day in Tucson. Therefore, it will probably be hot.

Deductive reasoning

Deductive reasoning is a method that proves a hypothesis or set of premises. The conclusion of a valid deductive argument will be true, given that the premises are true. Deductive reasoning utilizes logic to determine a conclusion.

Example:

> If a ding is a dong, then a ping is a pong.
> If a ping is a pong, then a ring is a ting.
> A ding is a dong.
> Therefore, a ring is a ting.
>
> This example is a deductive argument. A set of premises is used to determine a valid conclusion. In this example, the chain rule is illustrated. Specifically,
> $p \rightarrow q$
> $q \rightarrow r$
> p
> $$\overline{\quad\quad}$$
> $\therefore q$

Rules of logic

The rules of logic are related to deductive reasoning because one conclusion must be made, given a set of premises (or statements). A truth table may be used to determine the validity of an argument. In all cases, the determination of the conclusion is based on a top-down approach, whereby a set of premises yields a certain conclusion, albeit true or false, depending on the truth values of all premises.

Mathematical induction proof utilizing inductive reasoning

A mathematical induction proof utilizes inductive reasoning in its assumption that if $P(k)$ is true, then $P(k + 1)$ is also true. The induction hypothesis is $P(k)$. This step utilizes inductive reasoning because an observation is used to make the conjecture that $P(k + 1)$ is also true.

Example:

For all natural numbers, n, the sum is equal to $(n + 1) \left(\frac{n}{2}\right)$.

Show that $P(1)$ is true.
$1 = (1 + 1) \left(\frac{1}{2}\right)$.

Assume P(k) is true.
$1 + 2 + 3 + 4 + \cdots + k = (k + 1) \left(\frac{k}{2}\right)$.

This previous step is the inductive hypothesis. Using this hypothesis, it may be used to write the conjecture that $P(k + 1)$ is also true.

Formal reasoning

Formal reasoning, in mathematics, involves justification using formal steps and processes to arrive at a conclusion. Formal reasoning is utilized when writing proofs and using logic. For example, when applying logic, validity of a conclusion is determined by truth tables. A set of premises will yield a given conclusion. This type of thinking is formal reasoning. Writing a geometric proof also employs formal reasoning.

Example:

If a quadrilateral has four congruent sides, it is a rhombus.
If a shape is a rhombus, then the diagonals are perpendicular.
A shape is a quadrilateral.
Therefore, the diagonals are perpendicular.

This example employs the chain rule, shown below:
$p \rightarrow q$
$q \rightarrow r$
p
$\therefore r$

- 84 -

Informal reasoning

Informal reasoning, in mathematics, uses patterns and observations to make conjectures. The conjecture may be true or false. Several, or even many, examples may show a certain pattern, shedding light on a possible conclusion. However, informal reasoning does not provide a justifiable conclusion. A conjecture may certainly be deemed as likely or probable. However, informal reasoning will not reveal a certain conclusion.

Example:
- Mathematical Idea – Given a sequence that starts with 1 and increases by a factor of $\frac{1}{2}$, the limit of the sum will be 2.
- Informal Reasoning – The sum of 1 and $\frac{1}{2}$ is $1\frac{1}{2}$. The sum of 1, $\frac{1}{2}$, and $\frac{1}{4}$ is $1\frac{3}{4}$. The sum of 1, $\frac{1}{2}$, $\frac{1}{4}$, and $\frac{1}{8}$ is $1\frac{7}{8}$, Thus, it appears that as the sequence approaches infinity, the sum of the sequence approaches 2.

Problems

Use informal reasoning to justify the statement,
"If n is a whole number, then $n^2 + n + 1$ is odd."

Explain the reasoning steps used.

Given the sequence, 0, 1, 2, 3, 4, 5, 6, ..., evaluation of the expression, $n^2 + n + 1$, gives $0^2 + 0 + 1$, $1^2 + 1 + 1$, $2^2 + 2 + 1$, $3^2 + 3 + 1$, $4^2 + 4 + 1$, $5^2 + 5 + 1$, and $6^2 + 6 + 1$, or 1, 3, 7, 13, 21, 31, and 43, all of which are odd numbers. Thus, it appears that given any whole number, n, evaluation of the expression $n^2 + n + 1$ will yield an odd number.

Use formal reasoning to justify the statement,
"If a divides b, a divides c, and a divides d, then a divides the sum of b, c, and d."

Show the formal proof.

Direct Proof:
- Assume a divides b, a divides c, a divides d.

Given the definition of divides, a divides b indicates that there exists some integer, r, such that $b = a \cdot r$. Also, a divides c indicates that there exists some integer, s, such that $c = a \cdot s$. Finally, a divides d indicates that there exists some integer, t, such that $d = a \cdot t$. By substitution, the sum of b, c, and d may be written as $(a \cdot r) + (a \cdot s) + (a \cdot t)$. Factoring out an a gives $a(r + s + t)$. The factor $(r + s + t)$ is an integer, according to the closure property under addition. Thus, a divides the sum of b, c, and d.

Describe two different strategies for solving the problem,
"Kevin can mow the yard in 4 hours. Mandy can mow the same yard in 5 hours.
If they work together, how long will it take them to mow the yard?"

Two possible strategies both involve the use of rational equations to solve. The first strategy involves representing the fractional part of the yard mowed by each person in one hour and setting this sum equal to the ratio of 1 to the total time needed. The appropriate equation is $1/4 + 1/5 = 1/t$, which simplifies as $9/20 = 1/t$, and finally as $t = 20/9$. So, the time it will take them to mow the yard, when working together, is a little more than 2.2 hours. A second strategy involves representing the time needed for each person as two fractions and setting the sum equal to 1 (representing 1 yard). The appropriate equation is $t/4 + t/5 = 1$, which simplifies as $9t/20 = 1$, and finally as $t = 20/9$. This strategy also shows the total time to be a little more than 2.2 hours.

Describe two different strategies for solving the problem, "A car, traveling at
65 miles per hour, leaves Flagstaff and heads east on I-40. Another car,
traveling at 75 miles per hour, leaves Flagstaff 2 hours later, from the same
starting point and also heads east on I-40. After how many hours will the
second car catch the first car?"

One strategy might involve creating a table of values for the number of hours and distances for each car. The table may be examined to find the same distance traveled and the corresponding number of hours taken. Such a table is shown below:

Car A		Car B	
x (hours)	y (distance)	x (hours)	y (distance)
0	0	0	−150
1	65	1	−75
2	130	2	0
3	195	3	75
4	260	4	150
5	325	5	225
6	390	6	300
7	455	7	375
8	520	8	450
9	585	9	525
10	650	10	600
11	715	11	675
12	780	12	750
13	845	13	825
14	910	14	900
15	975	15	975

The table shows that after 15 hours, the distance traveled is the same. Thus, the second car catches up with the first car after a distance of 975 miles and 15 hours.

A second strategy might involve setting up and solving an algebraic equation. This situation may be modeled as $65x = 75(x - 2)$. This equation sets the distances traveled by each car equal to one another. Solving for x gives $x = 15$. Thus, once again, the second car will catch up with the first car after 15 hours.

The path of a ball, tossed into the air, from a given height, may be modeled with the function, $(x) = -2x^2 + 4x + 9$. Erica states that the ball will reach the ground after 4 seconds. Describe two different approaches for determining if her solution is, or is not, reasonable.

The ball will reach the ground when the x-value is 0. Thus, one approach involves finding a possible root for the function, by setting the equation equal to 0 and applying the quadratic formula. Doing so gives $0 = -2x^2 + 4x + 9$, where $a = -2$, $b = 4$, and $c = 9$. The positive x-value is approximately 3.3. Thus, her solution is not reasonable, since the ball would have reached ground level prior to 4 seconds. Another approach involves graphing the function and looking for the positive root. Since the root is less than 4, it can be determined that her solution is not reasonable.

Write a mixture word problem. Select and illustrate a strategy that may be used to solve the problem. State the solution.

Martin needs a 20% medicine solution. The pharmacy has a 5% solution and a 30% solution. He needs 50 mL of the solution. If the pharmacist must mix the two solutions, how many milliliters of 5% solution and 30% solution should be used?

To solve this problem, a table may be created to represent the variables, percentages, and total amount of solution. Such a table is shown below:

	mL solution	% medicine	Total mL medicine
5% solution	x	0.05	$0.05x$
30% solution	y	0.30	$0.30y$
Mixture	$x + y = 50$	0.20	$(0.20)(50) = 10$

The variable, x, may be rewritten as $50 - y$, so the equation, $0.05(50 - y) + 0.30y = 10$, may be written and solved for y. Doing so gives $y = 30$. So, 30 mL of 5% solution are needed. Evaluating the expression, $50 - y$ for a y-value of 30, shows that 20 mL of 30% solution are needed.

The relationship between Statistics Final Exam scores and Calculus Final Exam scores, for a random sample of students, is represented by the table below.

Statistics Final Exam Scores	Calculus Final Exam Scores
74	82
78	72
84	88
89	86
93	97

A teacher models this relationship with the function, $f(x) = 0.9x + 8.4$. Describe how well this model fits the situation. Explain the process used to evaluate the model.

The linear function is a good model for the relationship between the two sets of scores, as evidenced by a correlation coefficient of approximately 0.78. Any r-value that is 0.70 or higher indicates a strong correlation. The r^2-value is approximately 0.61. A residual plot of the data would show no clear pattern, indicating that a linear model would be appropriate. The residual plot is shown below:

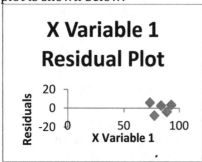

- 88 -

A residual plot does not show a clear pattern. Based on this information alone, explain how it may be determined whether or not the data may be represented by a linear model. Identify the appropriate model as linear or non-linear.

When a residual plot does not show a clear pattern (meaning the placement of the points are sporadic), it may be determined that the data represent a linear relationship. In other words, a linear model would be a good fit for the data. In order for the residual plot to indicate a non-linear model, the points would need to indicate some clear pattern. Examples of residual plots indicating a linear model and non-linear model are shown below:

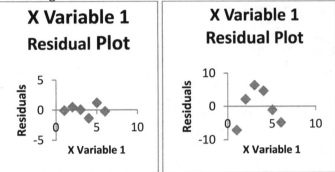

Carla wants to determine if the amount of her savings may best be modeled with a linear, cubic, other polynomial, or exponential function. Given some data points, describe at least two different strategies that she may employ to find the best fit function.

She may create a residual plot of the data to determine whether a linear model is appropriate. She may also use Excel or a graphing calculator to calculate and compare the r-values for different types of functions. This will show the best fit model. Note that some r-values may be quite similar, so the highest one will indicate the best fit model. There may be more than one appropriate model. She may also graph the data and visually compare the trendlines, deciding on the most appropriate fit.

The correlation between instructional strategy used and student achievement scores shows a correlation coefficient of approximately 0.84. Discuss whether a linear model is an appropriate function for this data.

The correlation coefficient is very high, thus a linear model would be very appropriate for modeling this data. Any correlation coefficient over 0.70 indicates a strong correlation, with one over 0.80 indicating a very strong correlation. The residual plot would not show any clear pattern. In other words, the points on the residual plot would be sporadic, for example, not showing a clear U-shaped or curved pattern. Shown below is a residual plot that represents data with an r-value of approximately 0.84:

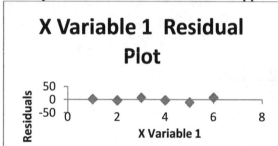

Notice that there is no clear pattern, and no curve or U-shape. Thus, this residual plot represents a linear relationship and may be modeled with a linear function.

Examples

Represent the data in the table below, using ordered pairs, a graph, and an equation.

x	y
0	6
1	2
2	−2
3	−6
4	−10

Multiple representations are shown below:

Ordered Pairs:

$(0, 6), (1, 2), (2, -2), (3, -6), (4, -10)$

- 90 -

The list of ordered pairs was created by substituting each x- and y-value, into the ordered pair form, (x, y).

Graph:

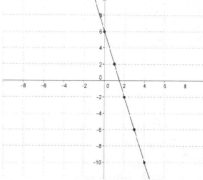

The graph was created by plotting each ordered pair and connecting the points with a line.

Equation:

$$y = -4x + 6$$

The slope of −4 was calculated from the table. The y-intercept is shown to be 6. Substituting the slope, m, and y-intercept, b, into the slope-intercept form of $y = mx + b$ gives $y = -4x + 6$.

Represent the triangular numbers, with three different representations.

The triangular numbers may be represented as follows:

List:

1, 3, 6, 10, 15, 21, ...

Diagram:

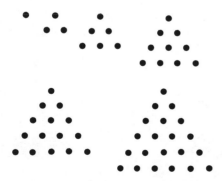

Equation:

$$a_n = \frac{n(n+1)}{2}$$

Explain how to represent the area under the normal curve, using z-scores and shading under the normal curve. Provide an example.

The area under a normal curve can be represented using one or two z-scores or a mean and a z-score. A z-score represents the number of standard deviations a score falls above, or below, the mean. A normal distribution table (z-table) shows the mean to z area, small portion area, and larger portion area, for any z-score from 0 to 4. The area between a mean and z-score is simply equal to the mean to z area. The area under the normal curve, between two z-scores, may be calculated by adding or subtracting the mean to z areas. An area above, or below, a z-score is equal to the smaller or larger portion area. The area may also be calculated by subtracting the mean to z area from 0.5, when looking at the smaller area, or adding the mean to z area to 0.5, when looking at the larger area.

Example:
- Suppose the class average on a final exam is 87, with a standard deviation of 2 points. Find the percentage of students who scored between 82 and 94.

Using z-scores and z-table alone:

$$z = \frac{82 - 87}{2} = -2.5$$
$$z = \frac{94 - 87}{2} = 3.5$$

The mean to z area for a z-score of −2.5 is 0.4938. The mean to z area for a z-score of 3.5 is 0.4998. The total area between these two z-scores is equal to the sum of 0.4938 and 0.4998, or 0.9936. Thus, 99.36% of the students scored between 82 and 94.

Represent the sine, cosine, and tangent of angles, measuring 30 degrees, 45 degrees, 60 degrees, and 90 degrees. Explain how the unit circle may be used to represent the exact values of the functions. Discuss how the unit circle may be used to find the values, when evaluating trig functions, given radian measures, as well.

The table below shows the values of each trig function:

Sine	Cosine	Tangent
$\sin(30°) = \dfrac{1}{2}$	$\cos(30°) = \dfrac{\sqrt{3}}{2}$	$\tan(30°) = \dfrac{1}{\sqrt{3}}$
$\sin(45°) = \dfrac{\sqrt{2}}{2}$	$\cos(45°) = \dfrac{\sqrt{2}}{2}$	$\tan(45°) = 1$
$\sin(60°) = \dfrac{\sqrt{3}}{2}$	$\cos(60°) = \dfrac{1}{2}$	$\tan(60°) = \sqrt{3}$
$\sin(90°) = 1$	$\cos(90°) = 0$	$\tan(90°)$ is undefined

The unit circle shows points, in the form, (x, y), on the circle, representing (cos, sin). Thus, each x-value represents the cosine of the measure, while each y-value represents the sine of the measure. The unit circle conveniently shows the degree measures and radian measures for each value. For example, in order to find the exact value of $\sin(30°)$, the degree measure may be located in Quadrant I, then the sine value will be the y-value, which is indeed $\frac{1}{2}$. Given $\sin\left(\frac{\pi}{6}\right)$, whereby theta ($\theta$) is represented in radians, the sine value will also be the y-value of the ordered pair, again shown to be $\frac{1}{2}$. These values may be checked by evaluating the functions, using a graphing calculator, in both degree and radian mode.

A professor wishes to invest $20,000 in a CD that compounds annually. The interest rate at his bank is 1.9%. He needs to know how many years it will take for his account to reach $50,000. Explain the process he should use to find the answer. Solve.

In order to solve, the compound interest formula should be evaluated for a future value of $50,000, principal of $20,000, rate of 0.019, and number of years of t. The exponential equation may then be solved by taking the logarithm of both sides. The process is shown below:

- $50,000 = 20,000\left(1 + \frac{0.019}{1}\right)^t$. Dividing both sides of the equation by 20,000 gives $2.5 = 1.019^t$.

Taking the logarithm of both sides gives $\log(2.5) = t\log(1.019)$. Dividing both sides of this equation by $\log(1.019)$ gives $t \approx 48.68$. Thus, after approximately 49 years, the professor's account will reach $50,000.

Suppose a new bacteria, after x days, shows a growth rate of 10%. The current count for the new bacteria strain is 100. Explain how to determine the number of days that will pass before the count reaches 1 million bacteria.

The problem may be solved by writing and solving an exponential growth function, in the form, $f(x) = a(1 + r)^x$, where $f(x)$ represents the future count, a represents the current count, r represents the growth rate, and x represents the time. Once the function is evaluated for a future count of 1,000,000, a current count of 100, and a growth rate of 0.10, the exponential equation may be solved by taking the logarithm of both sides.

The problem may be modeled with the equation, $1,000,000 = 100 \cdot (1.10)^x$. Dividing both sides of the equation by 100 gives $10,000 = 1.10^x$. Taking the logarithm of both sides gives $\log(10,000) = x \log(1.10)$. Dividing both sides of this equation by $\log(1.10)$ gives x ≈ 96.6. Thus, after approximately 97 days, the bacteria count will reach 1 million.

An object is tossed into the air. Write a function that may be used to model the height of the object, measured in feet, after x seconds have passed. Identify the number of seconds that will pass before the object reaches its maximum height. Identify the maximum height. Identify the number of seconds that will pass before the object reaches the ground. Explain how the answers were determined.

Possible function: $y = -x^2 + 6x + 6$. Three seconds will pass before the object reaches its maximum height. The function was graphed. The vertex of the graph shows an x-value of 3 and a y-value of 15. A table of values also shows a maximum y-value of 15, for a corresponding x-value of 3. Thus, after 3 seconds, the object will reach its maximum height of 15 feet. The positive x-intercept, or positive root, represents the point at which the object reaches the ground. Thus, after approximately 6.8 seconds, the object will reach the ground.

The Golden Ratio and the Fibonacci sequence

The Golden Ratio equals Phi, or 1.6180339887498948482…. The exact value of Phi is $(1 + \sqrt{5})/2$. The Golden Ratio is represented within the Fibonacci sequence. The Fibonacci sequence is 1, 1, 2, 3, 5, 8, 13, 21, 34, …, or a sequence whereby each term is equal to the sum of the two previous terms, for $n \geq 3$. The ratio of a term to the previous term approaches Phi, or the Golden Ratio, as the sequence approaches infinity.

A diagram used to illustrate the Golden Ratio is shown below:

When the ratio of x (the longer segment) to y (the shorter segment) is equal to the ratio of the sum of x and y (the whole segment) to x (the longer segment), the ratio equals Phi or the Golden Ratio. Thus, if a line segment is drawn, such that the ratio of the longer segment to the shorter segment equals the ratio of the whole segment to the longer segment, then the line segment illustrates the Golden Ratio, or approximately 1.618.

Problems

<u>Problem #1</u>

Represent the set of positive, even numbers, using recursive and explicit formulas. Represent the set of positive, odd numbers, using recursive and explicit formulas. Describe the types of functions represented by these sets.

Positive, even numbers:
- Recursive: $a_n = a_{n-1} + 2, n \geq 2$; Explicit: $a_n = 2n$

Positive, odd numbers:
- Recursive: $a_n = a_{n-1} + 2, n \geq 2$; Explicit: $a_n = 2n - 1$

Each set of numbers represents a linear function, with a constant rate of change of 2. The positive, even numbers represent a linear function that is proportional, whereas the positive, odd numbers represent a linear function that is not proportional. The set of even, positive numbers is represented by a function with a y-intercept of 0. The set of odd, positive numbers is represented by a function with a y-intercept of -1.

<u>Problem #2</u>

Andy opens a savings account with $10. During each subsequent week, he plans to double the amount deposited during the previous week. Represent his savings with a sequence. Write a function to represent his savings after x weeks. Explain the process used when determining the function.

Sequence: 10, 20, 40, 80, 160, …
Function: $a_n = 10 \cdot 2^{n-1}$

The sequence is a geometric sequence, with a common ratio of 2. All geometric sequences represent exponential functions. The nth term in any geometric sequence is represented by the general form, $a_n = a_1 \cdot r^{n-1}$, where a_n represents the value of the nth term, a_1 represents the value of the initial term, r represents the common ratio, and n represents the number of terms. Thus, substituting the initial value of 10 and common ratio of 2 gives the function, $a_n = 10 \cdot 2^{n-1}$.

Problem #3

A sales associate earns a 6% sales commission, plus a weekly salary of $400. Explain how the equation was determined. Suppose the sales associate sells $2,000 in merchandise in one week. Explain how to find the total earnings. Solve. Discuss whether or not the function represents a proportional relationship.

$f(x) = 0.06x + 400$; the sales commission of 6% represents the slope of the equation. The weekly salary of $400 is the flat rate, which represents the y-intercept of the equation. The total earnings for the week may be determined by evaluating the equation with an x-value of 2,000. The evaluation of the equation gives $f(x) = 0.06(2,000) + 400$, which yields $f(x) = 520$. The total earnings would be $520. The function does not represent a proportional relationship because the y-intercept is not 0. If the equation were to be graphed, the line would not pass through the origin, or the point, $(0, 0)$. When a linear graph does not pass through the origin, the function does not represent a proportional relationship.

Problem #4

Hannah writes the following equation: $f(x) = 30,000 \cdot (0.25)^x$. Describe a possible real-world situation that could be modeled by the equation. Evaluate the function for the set of natural numbers, and explain what the values would represent, as related to the context.

Since the equation is an exponential function, one possible real-world scenario would include the modeling of an initial mold spores count, a growth factor, and a current mold spores count. In this situation, it could be supposed that some bleach agent was used to eradicate the spores. Given this equation, the initial count would be 30,000, the rate of decay would be 0.25, x would represent the amount of time, perhaps in days, and f(x) would represent the current mold spores count. Evaluation of the function gives the sequence, 7500, 1875, 468.75, 117.19, 29.30, ... These values would represent the mold spores count, after 1, 2, 3, 4, and 5 days, respectively. The count for 0 days is the initial count, or y-intercept, of 30,000.

Problem #5

Suppose the initial population of a town was 1,200 people. The population growth is 5%. The current population is 2,400. Write a function that may be used to model the population, y, after x years. Find the number of years that have passed. Explain how the function and answer were determined and show the process used in solving.

Correct function: $2400 = 1200e^{0.05t}$.

The general form for population growth may be represented as $f(x) = ae^{rt}$, where $f(x)$ represents the current population, a represents the initial population, r represents the growth rate, and t represents the time. Thus, substituting the initial population, current population, and rate into this form gives the equation above.

The number of years that have passed were found by first dividing both sides of the equation by 1,200. Doing so gives $2 = e^{0.05t}$. Taking the natural logarithm of both sides gives $\ln(2) = ln(e^{0.05t})$. Applying the power property of logarithms, the equation may be rewritten as $\ln(2) = 0.05t \cdot$ ln (e), which simplifies as $\ln(2) = 0.05t$. Dividing both sides of this equation by 0.05 gives t $\approx$ 13.86. Thus, approximately 13.86 years passed.

Problem #6

Kim's savings is represented by the table below. Represent her savings, using an equation. Explain how the equation was found.

X (Number of Months)	Y (Total Savings, in Dollars)
2	1300
5	2050
9	3050
11	3550
16	4800

$$y = 250x + 800$$

The table shows a function with a constant rate of change, or slope, or 250. Given the points on the table, the slopes can be calculated as $(2050 - 1300)/(5 - 2)$, $(3050 - 2050)/(9 - 5)$, $(3550 - 3050)/(11 - 9)$, and $(4800 - 3550)/(16 - 11)$, each of which equals 250. Thus, the table shows a constant rate of change, indicating a linear function. The slope-intercept form of a linear equation is written as $y = mx + b$, where m represents the slope and b represents the y-intercept. Substituting the slope into this form gives $y = 250x + b$. Substituting corresponding x- and y-values from any point into this equation will give the y-intercept, or b. Using the point, (2, 1300), gives $1300 = 250(2) + b$, which simplifies as $b = 800$. Thus, her savings may be represented by the equation, $y = 250x + 800$.

Represent $\bar{A} \cap \bar{B}$, using a Venn diagram. Explain how the appropriate shading was determined.

The Venn diagram is shown below:

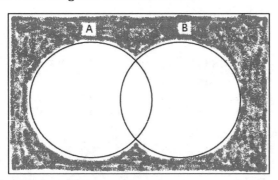

In order to correctly shade the Venn diagram, the complement of A must first be shaded. This would involve all regions not containing A. This includes part of B and the remainder of the universal set. Next, the complement of B may be shaded. This would involve all regions not containing B. This includes part of A and the remainder of the universal set. The intersection is the portion where the sets overlap. Thus, the overlapped shading is the portion of the universal set not containing the sets themselves, as shown above.

Problem #8

Suppose Rachel initially has $4,500. With each passing month, her account is one-half of what it was during the previous month. Show and describe the sequence, representing her balance. Write a function that may be used to model her account balance, after x months. Explain how the function was determined. Graph the function.

Sequence: 4500, 2250, 1125, 562.50, 281.25, ...

The sequence is geometric, since there is a common ratio of $\frac{1}{2}$. Thus, this sequence represents an exponential function. All geometric sequences represent exponential functions. (All arithmetic sequences represent linear functions.) The general form of a geometric sequence is $a_n = a_1 \cdot r^{n-1}$, where a_n represents the value of the nth term, a_1 represents the initial value, r represents the common ratio, and n represents the number of terms. Substituting the initial value of 4500 and common ratio of $\frac{1}{2}$ into this form gives $a_n = 4500 \cdot \left(\frac{1}{2}\right)^{n-1}$.

The graph of the function is shown below:

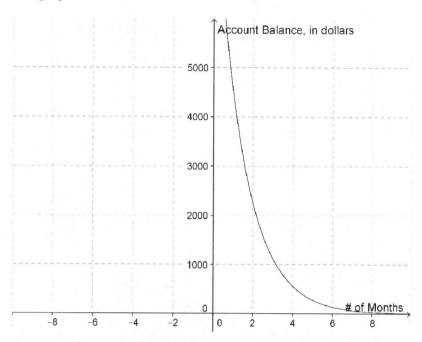

Problem #9

Use algebra tiles to complete the square for the expression, $x^2 + 8x$. Explain how the diagram shows the completion of the square.

Completing the square of $x^2 + 8x$ gives $x^2 + 8x + 16$, as shown by the 16 unit squares. Note. Each rod represents x. The diagram shows that $x^2 + 8x + 16$ is equal to $(x + 4)^2$. The side length of x^2 is x. The side length of each rod is 1. Thus, $(x + 4)(x + 4)$ also represents the area.

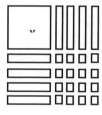

- 99 -

<u>Problem #10</u>

Create a small data set. Then, create a residual plot for the data. Explain why the residual plot provides more information about the linearity of the data than mere calculated residuals alone. Specifically describe what the residual plot shows and how it is interpreted.

Sample data set: (1, 63), (2, 75), (3, 63), (4, 98), (5, 93), (6, 91), (7, 94), (8, 80), (9, 99), (10, 75), (11, 99), (12, 98), (13, 87), (14, 80), (15, 64)

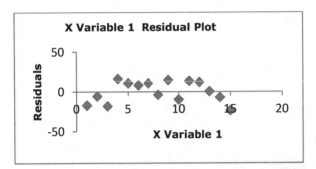

The residual plot shows a curved pattern. Thus, the plot indicates that the data are not linear and would not be appropriately modeled with a linear function. When a residual plot shows a curved or U-shaped pattern, a linear function would not be an appropriate function for modeling the data. When a residual plot shows no clear pattern or a sporadic placement of points, a linear function would be an appropriate model to use. The calculated residuals for the value at which the line of best fit is evaluated, for the given *x*-value.) This means that the difference in observed values minus predicted values is between 16 and –24, with the greatest difference having an absolute value of 24. These numbers alone are relative to the data set. Thus, a residual plot provides a much clearer analysis of the type of data represented.

Explain how a graphing calculator or Excel spreadsheet may be used to present the ideas of convergence and divergence. Decide if $\lim_{n\to\infty}(n^2 - 4n + 6)/(8n^2 + 2)$ represents convergence or divergence. If a limit exists, state the limit. If a limit does not exist, explain why.

The evaluation of an expression for consecutive values of n will show the pattern of the output, i.e., whether the values converge or diverge. In other words, a table of values or spreadsheet will show if the values grow without bound (diverge) or appear to converge to some single value.

This rational expression converges to a limit. This limit will approach 1/8, as n approaches infinity. Since the rational expression has the same leading powers in the numerator and denominator, the limit is simply the ratio of the coefficients of the leading terms, or 1/8.

The expression may be entered into a graphing calculator or spreadsheet. The table will show that as the x-values (or n-values) get larger and larger, the y-values (or output values) approach 0.125.

Two-way frequency table

A two-way frequency table quickly shows intersections and total frequencies. These values would have to be calculated from a manual list. The conditional probability, $P(B|A)$, read as "The probability of B, given A," is equal to $P(B \cap A)/A$. A two-way frequency table can quickly show these frequencies. Consider the table below:

	Cat	Dog	Bird	Total
Male	24	16	26	66
Female	32	12	20	64
Total	56	28	46	130

Find $P(Cat|Female)$. The two-way frequency table shows $C \cap F$ to be 32, while the total for female is 64. Thus, $P(Cat \mid Female) = 32/64 = 1/2$.

If the frequencies for male and each animal and frequencies for female and each animal had been listed, the total frequency for female would not have been as evident, at first glance.

Die roll simulator

A die roll simulator will show the results of n rolls of a die. The result of each die roll may be recorded. For example, suppose a die is rolled 100 times. All results may be recorded. The numbers of 1s, 2s, 3s, 4s, 5s, and 6s, may be counted. The experimental probability of rolling each number will equal the ratio of the frequency of the rolled number to the total number of rolls. As the number of rolls increases, or approaches infinity, the experimental probability will approach the theoretical probability of 1/6. Thus, the expected value for the roll of a die is shown to be $(1 \cdot 1/6) + (2 \cdot 1/6) + (3 \cdot 1/6) + (4 \cdot 1/6) + (5 \cdot 1/6) + (6 \cdot 1/6)$, or 3.5.

Nuances between a proper subset and a subset

A subset is simply a set that is contained within another set. The subset may or may not be equal to the set itself. If the subset is not equal to the set, the subset is said to be a proper subset. If the two sets are equal, meaning that all elements of the set are represented in the subset, the subset is simply called a subset, not a proper subset.

Given A = {4, 8, 12, 16, 20} and B = {2, 3, 4, 8, 12, 16, 20}, A is said to be a proper subset of B because the two sets are not equal. There are elements in B that are not contained in A. This would be denoted as $A \subset B$.

Now, suppose the following: A = {4, 8, 12, 16, 20} and B = {4, 8, 12, 16, 20}. A is equal to B. Thus, A is not a proper subset of B. This would be denoted as $A \subseteq B$.

Histogram and bar graph

A histogram shows frequencies for intervals of values. In other words, a histogram represents continuous data, or data that includes decimals or fractions. A bar graph simply represents frequencies for discrete values, or values that are distinct. An example of a discrete variable would be grade level. An example of a continuous variable would be weight of athletes. In order to tell if a graph is a histogram or a bar graph, the appearance of the bars and scale on the independent axis should be observed. If the bars are touching and intervals are shown, the graph is a histogram. If the bars are not touching and discrete values are given on the independent axis, the graph is a bar graph.

T-value vs. critical t-value

A t-value is the value that compares the difference in mean values to the standard deviation. The formula for t for one-sample t-test (comparing a sample mean to a population mean, when only the sample standard deviation is known) is $t = \frac{\bar{X} - \mu}{\frac{s}{\sqrt{n}}}$. It is the value that will be compared to the critical t-value, found in the t-distribution table. If the computed t-value has an absolute value that is greater than the critical t-value found in the table, for the desired level of significance and appropriate degrees of freedom, then it may be determined that a statistically significant difference exists between the groups. For example, suppose the following: a company claims to include 20 grams of beverage powder in each packet. A random sample of 30 packets shows a mean number of grams of 19.9, with a standard deviation of 0.1 grams. It may be determined if a statistically significant difference exists between the company's claim and the random sample mean by calculating a t-value and comparing it to the critical t-value for 29 degrees of freedom (n – 1). The t-value for this situation is approximately –5.4. Suppose the level of significance is 0.05. The critical t-value for 29 degrees of freedom, for a two-tailed test, would be 2.045. Since 5.4 is greater than 2.045, it may be declared that a statistically significant difference exists.

Many-to-one function and one-to-one function

A many-to-one function is a function whereby the relation is a function, but the inverse of the function is not a function. In other words, each element in the domain is mapped to one and only one element in the range. However, one or more elements in the range may be mapped to the same element in the domain. A one-to-one function is a function, whereby the inverse is also a function. In other words, each element in the domain is mapped to one and only one element in the range, and each element in the range is mapped to one and only one element in the domain. A graph of a many-to-one function would pass the vertical line test, but not the horizontal line test. A graph of a one-to-one function would pass both tests.

Mathematical Learning, Instruction, and Assessment

Cognitive theorists and constructivists

Constructivists believe that students may construct knowledge by themselves. In other words, students are actively engaged in the construction of their own knowledge. Students will assimilate and accommodate in order to build new knowledge, based on previous knowledge. Thus, in planning instruction based on constructivism, a teacher would focus on grouping designs, environment, problem-solving tasks, and inclusion of multiple representations. The goal in such a classroom would be for students to construct knowledge on their own. There are different levels of constructivism, including weak constructivism and radical constructivism.

Cognitivists differ from constructivists in that they believe that active exploration is important in helping students make sense of observations and experiences. However, the students are not expected to invent or construct knowledge by themselves. They are only expected to make sense of the mathematics. In planning instruction based on cognitivism, a teacher would employ similar methods to those discussed above, with the focus on active exploration. Students would do a lot of comparisons of mathematical methods in making sense of ideas.

Constructivism

Three types of constructivism are weak constructivism, social constructivism, and radical constructivism. Weak constructivists believe that students construct their own knowledge, but also accept certain preconceived notions or facts. Social constructivists believe that students construct knowledge by interacting with one another and holding discussions and conversations. Radical constructivists believe that all interpretations of knowledge are subjective, based on the individual learner. In other words, there is no real truth; it is all subjective. Classroom instructional planning based on a weak constructivist viewpoint might involve incorporation of some accepted theorems and definitions, while continuing to plan active explorations and discussions. Planning based on a social constructivist viewpoint might involve group activities, debates, discussion forums, etc. Planning based on a radical constructivist viewpoint would involve activities that are open-ended, where there is more than one correct answer. The problems would invite more than one correct answer.

Project-based learning

Project-based learning is learning that centers on the solving of a problem. Students learn many different ideas by solving one "big" problem. For example, for a unit on sine and cosine functions, a teacher may design a problem whereby the students are asked to model a real-world phenomenon using both types of functions. Students must investigate the effects of changes in amplitude, period, shifts, etc., on the graphs of the functions. Students will also be able to make connections between the types of functions when modeling the same phenomenon. Such a problem will induce high-level thinking.

Project-based learning is derived from constructivist theory, which contends that students learn by doing and constructing their own knowledge.

Cooperative learning

Cooperative learning simply means that students will learn by cooperating with one another. Students will be placed into groups of a size determined by the teacher. With such an approach, students work together to succeed in learning. Students may work together to learn a topic, complete an assignment, or compete with other groups.

Examples of cooperative learning include Think-Pair-Share and Jigsaw. Think-Pair-Share is a cooperative learning strategy that involves thinking about some given topic, sharing ideas, thoughts, or questions with a partner, and then sharing the partner discussion with the whole group. For example, in the mathematics classroom, a teacher may ask the class to think about the meaning of a proportional relationship. Each student would think for a set period of time, share ideas with a partner, and then each partner group would share their ideas regarding the meaning of proportionality. Jigsaw is another cooperative learning strategy that involves dividing among each group member reading material or ideas to be learned. Each student will then read his or her information, summarize it, and share the findings or ideas with the group. In mathematics, students might be given information on modeling with cosine and sine functions. Students could then share what they learned about real-world phenomena modeled by each. Different students may also be assigned to read in-depth material on amplitude, period, shifts, etc.

Control strategies

"Control strategies" is another name for "metacognitive learning strategies," which indicate any strategy that promotes a learner's awareness of his or her level of learning. With such strategies, the student will work to determine what he or she knows and does not know regarding a subject. Possible control strategies are thinking, self-regulation, and discussing ideas with peers.

Example:
- A student may discover his or her level of "knowing" about functions by keeping a journal of any questions he or she might have regarding the topic. The student may list everything that he or she understands, as well as aspects not understood. As the student progresses through the course, he or she may go back and reconfirm any correct knowledge and monitor progress on any previous misconceptions.

Memorization and elaboration strategies

Memorization is simply a technique whereby rote repetition is used to learn information. Elaboration strategies involve the connection of new information to some previously learned information. In mathematics, for example, students may use elaboration strategies when learning how to calculate the volume of a cone, based on their understood approach for calculating the volume of a cylinder. The student would be making connections in his or her mind between this new skill and other previously acquired skills. A memorization technique would simply involve memorization of the volume of a cone formula, as well as ways to evaluate the formula.

Prior knowledge

Three ways of activating students' prior knowledge are concept mapping, visual imagery, and comparing and contrasting. With concept mapping, a student would detail and connect all known aspects of a mathematics topic. Ideas would be grouped into subgroups. Such an approach would allow a student to see what he or she does not know, prompting the activation of any prior knowledge on the subject. Visual imagery is simply the use of any pictures or diagrams to promote activation of prior knowledge. For example, giving a picture of Pascal's triangle would likely activate students' prior knowledge regarding the Binomial Theorem. Comparing and contrasting means that the student will compare and contrast ideas or approaches. For example, a student might be given a mapping of an inverse function. He or she could then compare and contrast this mapping to a known mapping of a function, in order to decide how they are the same and different. This would activate a student's prior understanding of functions and the definition thereof.

Three methods for ascertaining, or assessing, students' prior knowledge are portfolios, pre-tests, and self-inventories. Portfolios are simply a compilation of prior student activity related to mathematics topics. For example, a portfolio might show a student's work with transforming functions. Pre-tests are designed to measure a student's understanding of mathematics topics that will be taught in the course during the year. Self-inventories are just what the name implies: inventories that ask the students to name, list, describe, and explain information understood about various mathematics topics.

Once a teacher has assessed students' level of prior knowledge regarding some mathematics topic, he or she may use that information to scaffold the instruction. In other words, the teacher may decide to further break down the mathematics material into more integral parts. Exact processes or steps may be shown, including justification for using certain properties or theorems. More examples may be shown, while including examples of many different variations of problems, in order to ensure that students are not simply memorizing one approach that will be incorrectly applied to any problem of that sort. The teacher may also decide that more group work, peer cooperation, and discussion are needed.

For example, suppose a teacher determines that students have very little understanding of logic and valid arguments. The teacher may decide to re-teach the creation of truth tables, including truth values for intersections and "if p, then q" statements. The teacher may also decide to re-teach how a truth table may be used to show if an argument is valid. Students may be placed into groups and asked to determine the validity of several simple arguments. Once students understand the concept, they may move on to more rigorous arguments, including equivalence relations.

Concept whereby usage of manipulatives would increase conceptual understanding

Understanding of how to solve one-variable equations would certainly be enhanced by using rods and counters. With this manipulative, the rod would represent the variable, or x, while the counters would represent the constants on each side of the equation. A sample diagram of the equation, $x + 4 = 8$, is shown below. Note that the vertical line represents the equals sign.

In order to solve the equation (and isolate x), four counters may be removed from each side of the mat. This process is shown below:

Now, the final illustration is:

Thus, the solution is $x = 4$. The manipulative helps students understand the meaning of the subtraction property of equality in action, without simply memorizing its meaning.

Problems

<u>Problem #1</u>

Explain how an understanding of the area under the normal curve may be supported by using a graphing calculator. Provide a sample problem and describe the steps involved in solving, using both a manual approach and a technological approach.

The area under the normal curve may be found by calculating z-scores for certain endpoint values. The mean to z areas for these z-scores may be used to find the area. A graphing calculator may use the normalpdf function and ShadeNorm function in order to show the same area under the normal curve, between two values. Consider the following problem: The class average on a statistics exam is 90, with a standard deviation of 4 points. Find the percentage of students who scored above 87 on the exam.

This problem may be solved manually by first calculating the z-score.

$$z = \frac{87 - 90}{4} = \frac{-3}{4}$$

Since the score falls below the mean, the area above the score will equal the sum of 0.5 (or the area of one-half of the normal curve) and the mean to z area, which is 0.2734. Thus, the area above the z-score of −0.75 is 0.7734. The percentage of students who scored above 87 was 77.34%.

This problem may also be solved by using the graphing calculator:
1. Enter normalpdf(x, 0, 1) into the y = screen. (This represents the normal curve having a mean of 0 and standard deviation of 1.)
2. Choose 2nd Vars, ShadeNorm(.
3. Enter ShadeNorm(87,100,90,4). (This represents the lower bound, upper bound, mean, and standard deviation.)
4. Record the area of approximately 0.77.
5. Thus, the calculator also shows that approximately 77% of the students scored above an 87.

Problem #2

Describe how the understanding of derivative and anti-derivative may be enhanced/supported using a graphing calculator. Provide an example and show how to solve, using a manual approach and technological approach.

The derivative of an expression is the slope of a tangent line to the curve, at a specific point. The anti-derivative of an expression is the inverse operation of the derivative. Taking the derivative of the anti-derivative will give the original expression. The derivative and anti-derivative can be calculated manually as shown below:

Given $f(x) = 3x^2 + 8x + 4$, the derivative is $f(x) = 6x + 8$. The anti-derivative is $f(x) = x^3 + 4x^2 + 4x$. Thus, evaluation of the derivative and anti-derivative for an x-value of 2 gives $f(x) = 20$ and $f(x) = 32$, respectively. The student can confirm his or her derivative and anti-derivative expressions by evaluating the graphed functions for the same x-value. If the expressions were correctly determined, then evaluation of the derivative and anti-derivative for the x-value should give the same y-value, for each.

Using the graphing calculator, the derivative and anti-derivative for a given point may be evaluated by entering the expression into the y = screen, graphing the function, selecting 2nd Trace, and then choosing dy/dx and $\int f(x)dx$. After selecting the derivative or anti-derivative, the x-value may be typed. Evaluation of the derivative or anti-derivative for that x-value will appear on the screen.

Piaget's cognitive development theory

Piaget's cognitive development theory is aligned with constructivism. In fact, constructivism is built on his ideas. Piaget's cognitive development theory indicates that students actively participate in the construction of their own knowledge via assimilation and accommodation. Current cognitive theorists do not believe that students have to construct their own knowledge, but instead that they only have to make sense of what they are observing.

The four stages of learning, as developed by Piaget, are sensorimotor, preoperational, concrete operational, and formal operational. The defined stages show the progression from concrete thinking to abstract thinking. In other words, a child would need an object to understand properties, in the first stage. By the fourth stage, the child would be able to think abstractly, without some concrete form. In mathematics, this idea might be illustrated by first working with diagrams and manipulatives of numbers and then later writing symbolic forms of the numbers, including the numerals. This would illustrate the progression from 0 to 7 years. In the years of 11 to adulthood, much deeper abstraction is utilized. For example, people would be able to discuss functions and general properties, without looking at any concrete graphs or representations.

Progression that a student undergoes as he or she learns mathematics

When learning mathematics, students begin with concrete representations and ideas. Later, students are able to abstract meaning and make generalizations. Students will also be asked to apply abstract ideas from one topic to another mathematics topic. In other words, students would move from concrete representations, ideas, and facts to symbolic representations and generalizations. Piaget outlined such a progression in his general four stages of cognitive learning. For example, a student may first learn about solving equations by using a balance scale. After the student understands the process, he or she can solve alone, using the symbolic equations. He or she would also be able to describe the process for solving any equation.

Direct instruction versus student-centered instruction

Direct instruction is instruction whereby the teacher delivers all content knowledge to be learned, and students, more or less, passively listen. The teacher employs a step-by-step instruction method for learning content. Student-centered instruction is learning whereby the teacher serves as a facilitator of learning and students actively participate in their own learning. Research has shown that students show a higher level of procedural and conceptual understanding when learning in a student-centered approach. Direct instruction might be more appropriate when teaching basic or fundamental theorems. Student-centered learning might be more appropriate when helping students make connections or develop higher-level thinking regarding a topic.

Cooperative learning task versus traditional task

Think-Pair-Share is an activity whereby a topic is first given for consideration on an individual basis. Next, the students are arranged in pairs and asked to discuss the topic (e.g., any questions, comments, generalizations, etc.). Finally, each pair will contribute to a whole-class discussion on the topic.

In mathematics, students would likely develop a higher level of understanding by using such an activity as Think-Pair-Share when learning about trigonometric functions. For example, students might be asked to consider different real-world situations that may be modeled with sine and cosine functions. Students could individually make a list and then share with a partner. Each partner group could then contribute to a whole class list. This list could be used as a reference sheet.

Implementing technology in classroom instruction

Technology may be implemented in the mathematics classroom in many ways. For example, Excel may be used to perform regressions, calculate lines of best fit, calculate correlation coefficients, plot residuals, show convergence or divergence of a sequence, etc. Calculators may be used to evaluate and graph functions, find area under the normal curve, calculate combinations and permutations, perform statistical tests, etc. Graphing software, such as GeoGebra, may be used to graph and explore many shapes and functions. Students may also use it to graph reflections, rotations, translations, and dilations.

Modifying instruction to accommodate English-language learners

In mathematics specifically, instruction may be modified to include illustrations of ideas, in addition to given words. Audio may also be included for problem tasks. English-language learners may also be grouped with other fluent English-speaking students in order to assist with learning of the mathematics topic. Students will be able to hear the conversation, in addition to seeing the topic in print. In addition, problems may be broken down into smaller pieces, which can help the student focus on one step at a time. Further, additional one-on-one time with the teacher may be needed, whereby the teacher reads aloud and illustrates examples to be learned.

Effective learning environment for ELL students

Characteristics of an effective learning environment for ELL students include creation of a low threshold for anxiety, use of pictures to teach vocabulary and mathematics ideas, implementation of graphic organizers, explicit teaching of vocabulary words, and use of active learning strategies. The latter two are extremely important, since ELL students need to learn exact terms and exact definitions while also engaging with fellow students, as opposed to sitting alone at a desk. Research completed by professors at the University of Houston and University of California list collaborative learning, use of multiple representations, and technology integration as important facets of an effective learning environment for ELL students (Waxman & Tellez, 2002).

Mathematics question that is closed-ended and then rewritten in an open-ended manner

Closed-Ended:
- Look at the graph of $y = x^2 + 2$. Decide if the graph represents a function.

Open-Ended:
- Provide an example of an equation that represents a function. Provide an example of an equation that does not represent a function. Explain how the graphs of the two equations compare to one another.

The first question will elicit a simple, straightforward response, or "Yes, it is a function."

The second question prompts the student to come up with two equations and then describe how the graphs of the two equations would compare. There is more than one possible answer, and the student has to make a comparison as well.

Good questioning response techniques

A few good questioning response techniques are:
1. Make sure the wait time is sufficient;
2. Do not include leading prompts within questions;
3. Ask more questions based on student answers;
4. Confirm or restate correct student comments.

The key to good questioning response techniques is to show the student that his or her comments are important and to connect those comments to other student comments. The student should feel that he or she has made a contribution to the community of learners. A teacher should always ask a meaningful, thought-provoking question and provide sufficient time for the student to provide a meaningful and well-thought-out response. Student answers should lead to more questions and ideas and not serve as an endpoint.

NCTM categories of questions that teachers should ask

The Professional Standards describe five categories of questions that teachers should ask. These categories are: 1) working together to make sense of problems; 2) individually making sense of problems; 3) reasoning about mathematics; 4) providing conjectures about mathematics; and 5) making connections within and outside of mathematics. Sample questions include "What does this mean?," "How can you prove that?," and "What does this relate to?". Categories 4 and 5 are high level and include questions that prompt students to invent ideas and make meaningful connections.

Accountants and mathematical modeling

Accountants use mathematical modeling in a variety of ways. For example, an accountant models the future value of a certificate of deposit (CD) using the compound interest formula. An accountant also may fit a regression line to a client's overall savings over x years. An accountant may model tax payments with residual plots. Accountants may use past income tax returns to predict future tax expenses. Accountants may compare rates of return when investing in different mutual funds, by fitting and comparing regression lines.

Scientists and functions

Scientists use functions to model real-world phenomena. For example, scientists use quadratic functions to model the height of an object tossed into the air or dropped from a certain height. Scientists use sine and cosine functions to model real-world occurrences such as the depth of water at various times of the day, the movement of a pendulum, etc. Scientists use exponential functions to analyze and predict the number of bacteria present after x amount of time. Scientists also use functions when analyzing the time it takes a rocket to reach a destination.

Making mathematics relevant to students' lives

Teachers can make mathematics relevant to students, using a variety of strategies. Teachers may include items relevant and pertinent to students within question stems, such as including "iPad," "apps," and video game names. Teachers should pose questions that are similar to what students may have asked themselves, such as, "If I invest this much money in an account and save for x years, after how many years will I have y dollars?" Teachers should include real-world problems to solve, and not simply include rote solving of equations. Students should know what sorts of scenarios may be modeled with rational expressions. Many researchers believe that curricula should be centered on the "real world," with all facets of mathematics learning spawning from that center. In other words, students often know how to convert a decimal to a percentage, but when reading *The Wall Street Journal*, they may not be able to interpret a percentage yield.

Assessment tool

A mathematics assessment tool is used to assess a student's prior knowledge, current knowledge, skill set, procedural knowledge, conceptual understanding, depth of understanding, and ability to make abstractions and generalizations. Perhaps the most important purpose of such a tool is to help the student develop and modify instruction. A teacher may determine that students are ready to surpass the current lesson or need it to be much more scaffolded. A teacher may also use the assessment to track students' progress. For example, a portfolio might show students' initial understanding of functions and end with their work with function modeling.

When a teacher needs to decide on an appropriate assessment tool, he or she needs to consider the purpose of the assessment. For example, if the purpose of an assessment is to direct the instruction, a pre-test may be a good assessment to use. If the purpose of the assessment is to determine the level of student understanding, then a whole-class discussion may be desired. If the purpose of an assessment is to assess student understanding of a unit of material, then an exam would be appropriate. If a teacher wishes to analyze student understanding and ability to abstract knowledge, then a performance assessment may be used. If a teacher wishes to check off skills mastered by students, then a checklist would be appropriate.

Valid test

A test is valid if it tests what it is supposed to test. In other words, a test is valid if it appropriately covers the material it is supposed to cover. For example, a topic not taught in class should not be included on a valid test. In order to construct a valid test, a teacher should make a list of all standards covered during that time period. The teacher should also closely mirror the design of problems examined in class, for homework, and in group discussions. Finally, the teacher should make sure that there is an even balance of questions to cover all of the material.

Valid exam

In order to select a valid exam, a teacher should make sure that the test aligns with the objectives and standards covered in the unit. The teacher should also make sure that the test problems are similar to those covered during class time. The teacher should make sure the percentages of questions devoted to each objective are balanced. In order for a test to be valid, it must be reliable, meaning that it produces similar results with different groups. A teacher may wish to check the validity and reliability results of an exam.

In general, an exam is considered invalid if it does not measure what it is supposed to measure. The exam may include questions from another unit. It may include questions with different wording techniques, making it much more difficult. The exam may include representations different from those covered in class. An invalid exam would not be reliable, meaning the results would not be consistent with different administrations of the exam. Biased questions and wording may also make an exam invalid.

Assessing students' understanding of what has been taught

In order to assess thought processes, open-ended questions are needed. The teacher may wish to have students write an essay, write entries in a mathematics journal, undergo a performance task, or participate in a debate or discussion. The teacher may also design a pre-test that includes all constructed response questions. In particular, a performance task requires students to justify solutions, which provide the teacher with insight into students' understanding and reasoning. In general, the assessment should include questions that ask students to make abstractions and justify their thinking.

Testing issue

<u>A student claims that an exam is more difficult and includes more content than what was presented in class. How might a teacher determine if the student's claim is true?</u>
The teacher would need to make a list of all objectives and standards covered during the time period. The teacher would also need to compile all problems and examples covered in class and as homework. Finally, the teacher would need to do a careful analysis of the wording of the problems covered in class and as homework. If any of these items are not aligned to the exam, the teacher would need to go back and re-teach the material, using the created test as a guide for instruction.

Performance task

A performance task allows the teacher to assess process as well as product, meaning that a teacher can assess students' thought processes as well as their final answer. The level of student learning will be much clearer when reviewing a performance task. A performance task goes beyond a multiple-choice format, allowing for oral and tactile-kinesthetic performances. Furthermore, a performance task may combine several mathematics concepts into one assessment instrument. This type of assessment often includes real-world problems, which helps the student connect mathematics to the outside world.

Formative and summative assessments

Formative assessments are those given during the learning process. Formative assessments provide the teacher with information related to a student's progress at various stages throughout a time period. Formative assessments are used to modify instruction as needed. In other words, formative assessments inform instruction. Summative assessments are those given at the end of a learning period. Summative assessments serve to measure the cumulative knowledge gained. Examples of formative assessments include quizzes, checklists, observations, and discussion. Examples of summative assessments include exams, portfolios, performance tasks, and standardized tests.

Four formative assessments include quizzes, checklists, observations, and discussion. Quizzes are often short assessments that may include multiple-choice items, short response items, or essay items. Quizzes are often administered following presentation of a portion of a mathematics unit. Checklists include a list of skills or concepts that should be mastered or understood. A teacher will check off all items mastered by a student. Observations are informal means of assessing students' understanding of a topic. A teacher may observe students' questions, engagement, and performance on projects. Discussion is another informal formative assessment. Discussions, both in groups and whole-class formats, allow the teacher to analyze students' thinking.

Four summative assessments include exams, portfolios, performance tasks, and standardized tests. Exams may include closed-ended or open-ended questions. Exams may be administered after each unit, semester, or at the end of the year. Portfolios include tasks created by a student and may include writing pieces and other large projects. Although the portfolio contains formative work, the tool itself may be used as a summative assessment piece. Performance tasks are large-scale problems that include many different components that relate to some big idea. For example, a student may be asked to formulate a plan for modeling a real-world phenomenon with a sine function. The student may be asked to explain how the function would change, given changes to the amplitude, period, shifts, etc. The student may then explain how these components would need to change to fit a new function. Standardized tests are tests that compare a student's performance to that of other students. They are often given at the end of the school year.

Scoring rubric

A strong rubric will include unique performance criteria for each bullet. In other words, a portion of one criteria statement should not be included in a portion of another criteria statement. Each criteria statement should be clearly delineated, describing exactly what the student must be able to do. Furthermore, a strong rubric will often have scoring options, ranging from 0 to 4. When designing the rubric, it is helpful to create a model student response that will warrant each rubric score. It is also helpful to provide a space to provide feedback to students.

Enhancing student understanding

In order for an assessment to enhance student understanding, it should provide an opportunity for the student to learn something. The assessment should be a learning opportunity for the student. It should prompt the student to think deeper about a mathematics topic. In other words, the student should think, "Okay. I understand this. I wonder how the process/solution would change if I did this." The assessment might prompt the student to ask deeper questions in the next class session or complete research on a certain topic. In order to create such an assessment, open-ended and challenging questions should be included on the exam. The exam should not consist of simple, lower-level, one-answer questions.

Testing mathematical misconceptions

In order to design such an assessment, the teacher should include mathematical error-type problems, whereby the student must look at a solution process or conjecture and determine if he or she agrees, of if and where an error occurred. The student would need to identify the error, correct it, and explain why it was erroneous. The assessment should include a variety of mathematical misconceptions. One solution process may include more than one error. A teacher may also simply ask students to participate in a collaborative learning activity, whereby the students must share ideas and thoughts regarding a new mathematical topic.

Assessing prior knowledge

Such a pre-test must not include any leading prompts. It should include open-ended and constructed-response items as well. A pre-test with solely multiple-choice items will not be sufficient, since a student has the option of guessing. The test should include higher-level questions that require connections within the field of mathematics. In other words, the questions should not all be mutually exclusive. They should build on one another. Finally, the test might include student error problems as well.

Assessing both procedural knowledge and conceptual understanding

The assessment should include rote, algorithmic-type problems, as well as those that ask the student to utilize higher-level thinking, abstractions, and generalizations. The test should include open-ended, constructed-response-type problems. A performance task is an excellent assessment for assessing a student's ability to solve a problem, while also examining the student's thought processes, rationales, etc. In order to assess both types of understanding, the assessment will need to ask students to justify and explain solutions. In other words, the assessments should include questions at both ends of Bloom's Taxonomy.

Pre-test and post-test

A post-test should be exactly the same as an administered pre-test. If the teacher is to compare the results of a post-test to a pre-test, then the test and testing conditions should be identical. The pre-test assesses students' prior knowledge, while a post-test assesses students post knowledge. Comparing the results, side by side, allows the teacher to track student progress. The teacher may wish to add additional questions to the post-test, but the original questions should remain.

Assessment that will show what students do and do not know

The teacher should include questions that are straightforward, involve errors, require justification, and require shown work. A student self-assessment is one such tool that would show misconceptions, understood material, and advanced knowledge. The assessment should include more than multiple-choice questions. Designing a performance assessment with scaffolded questions, whereby only one solution may be found based on a previous answer, will also show students' exact level of understanding. A debate format is one type of assessment whereby the teacher will be able to see a student's level of understanding, as he or she seeks to respond with a rebuttal.

Assessment to hone in on any error patterns evident in students' work

A portfolio would be an excellent assessment for monitoring any student error patterns. The teacher would be able to track student errors as the course progressed. The teacher would be given insight into how, and if, errors improved, or if some knowledge was acquired but other knowledge was still incorrect. The portfolio might include a series of similar questions related to a certain topic. For example, a portfolio may include function transformation questions. A student's ability to transform functions may be tracked, starting with simple linear functions and ending with complex sine functions.

Components that must be present in an assessment that supports student learning

The assessment must require students to think deeper than what they have covered in class. It should prompt them to make connections between topics. It should invite different ways of thinking about problem solving. In other words, the student may think, "Okay. I have seen a similar version in class. This problem is slightly different, in that the parabola is shifted left. This is the opposite of shifting right, so I will add the constant to the x-term." The assessment will thus solidify the student's understanding of how to shift any function.

Using assessment results of assessments given to ELL learners in order to modify instruction

The teacher would be able to see if language itself is a barrier in learning. In other words, if the group of ELL students, as a whole, show difficulty with a mathematics topic, the teacher may deduce that the content was not clear due to minimal supporting pictures, diagrams, and auditory support. The teacher may decide to reteach the lesson, using more visual cues, verbal pronunciations, explicit vocabulary usage, and peer-group placement. Collaborative learning may be employed.

Questions that a teacher may ask after reviewing the results of an administered exam

The teacher may ask the following:
1. Did I cover the content in an explicit manner?
2. Did I show plenty of examples?
3. Did I use multiple representations when teaching the concepts?
4. Did I design instruction such as to accommodate all modes of learning?
5. Was the test valid?
6. Did students have an adequate amount of time to complete the test?
7. Why did some groups of students score lower or higher?
8. Did any biased questions affect the results?

How focus on career and college readiness affects assessment and instructional design

The focus on college and career-readiness standards prompts publishers and teachers to utilize more real-world problems in instruction and assessments. The focus in mathematics classrooms is shifting to more real-world, cumulative problems that require understanding of many different mathematics concepts in order to solve. Problems are related to science, finance, medicine, etc. The focus includes the ability to apply the algorithms to many different career situations. In summary, the recent focus shifts the instructional design to an application-based status.

Role of assessment in a classroom focused on cognitive instruction

A cognitively guided classroom would be similar to a constructivist classroom, in that active participation would be present. However, in a cognitive classroom (as advocated by current cognitive theorists), students are not required to invent their own knowledge. Instead, they must simply make sense of what they are observing and experiencing. They may be assisted by the teacher. Thus, the role of an assessment in such a classroom is to ascertain student thought processes. Such an assessment would ask students to describe thinking and perhaps make connections to other mathematics topics. The assessment must ascertain students' reasoning abilities.

Instructional cycle described by a learning theorist

The 5E Learning Model is based on the thinking of Jean Piaget. It is a constructivist learning model. Piaget believed that students construct their own knowledge via active participation and experiences. Problem solving is integral to student learning. The cycle is listed as engagement, exploration, explanation, elaboration, and evaluation. Thus, with active engagement and exploration, the student is able to develop his or her own explanation, use assimilation and accommodation to make sense of the information, and then evaluate the material and make conjectures, etc.

Scientific Inquiry and Processes

Scientific process

Perhaps the most important skill in science is that of observation. A scientist must be able to take accurate data from his experimental setup or from nature without allowing bias to alter the results. Another important skill is hypothesizing. A scientist must be able to combine his knowledge of theory and of other experimental results to logically determine what should occur in his own tests. The data-analysis process requires the twin skills of ordering and categorizing. Gathered data must be arranged in such a way that it is readable and readily shows the key results. A skill that may be integrated with the previous two is comparing. A scientist should be able to compare his own results with other published results. He must also be able to infer, or draw logical conclusions, from his results. He must be able to apply his knowledge of theory and results to create logical experimental designs and determine cases of special behavior. Lastly, a scientist must be able to communicate his results and his conclusions. The greatest scientific progress is made when scientists are able to review and test one another's work and offer advice or suggestions.

Scientific method of inquiry

The scientific method of inquiry is a general method by which ideas are tested and either confirmed or refuted by experimentation. The first step in the scientific method is formulating the problem that is to be addressed. It is essential to clearly define the limits of what is to be observed, since that allows for a more focused analysis. Once the problem has been defined, it is necessary to form a hypothesis. This educated guess should be a possible solution to the problem that was formulated in the first step. The next step is to test that hypothesis by experimentation. This often requires the scientist to design a complete experiment. The key to making the best possible use of an experiment is observation. Observations may be quantitative, that is, when a numeric measurement is taken, or they may be qualitative, that is, when something is evaluated based on feeling or preference. This measurement data will then be examined to find trends or patterns that are present. From these trends, the scientist will then draw conclusions or make generalizations about the results, intended to predict future results. If these conclusions support the original hypothesis, the experiment is complete and the scientist will publish his conclusions to allow others to test them by repeating the experiment. If they do not support the hypothesis, the results should then be used to develop a new hypothesis, which can then be verified by a new or redesigned experiment.

Experimental design

Designing relevant experiments that allow for meaningful results is not a simple task. Every stage of the experiment must be carefully planned to ensure that the right data can be safely and accurately taken. Ideally, an experiment should be controlled so that all of the conditions except the ones being manipulated are held constant. This helps to ensure that the results are not skewed by unintended consequences of shifting conditions. A good example of this is a placebo group in a drug trial. All other conditions are the same, but that group is not given the medication. In addition to proper control, it is important that the experiment be designed with data collection in mind. For instance, if the quantity to be measured is temperature, there must be a temperature device such as a thermocouple integrated into the experimental setup. While the data are being collected, they should periodically be checked for obvious errors. If there are data points that are orders of magnitude from the expected value, then it might be a good idea to make sure that no experimental errors are being made, either in data collection or condition control. Once all the data have been gathered, they must be analyzed. The way in which this should be done depends on the type of data and the type of trends observed. It may be useful to fit curves to the data to determine if the trends follow a common mathematical form. It may also be necessary to perform a statistical analysis of the results to determine what effects are significant. Finally, the data should be presented in a clear and logical fashion.

Scientific statements

Hypotheses are educated guesses about what is likely to occur, and are made to provide a starting point from which to begin design of the experiment. They may be based on results of previously observed experiments or knowledge of theory, and follow logically forth from these. Assumptions are statements that are taken to be fact without proof for the purpose of performing a given experiment. They may be entirely true, or they may be true only for a given set of conditions under which the experiment will be conducted. Assumptions are necessary to simplify experiments; indeed, many experiments would be impossible without them. Scientific models are mathematical statements that describe a physical behavior. Models are only as good as our knowledge of the actual system. Often models will be discarded when new discoveries are made that show the model to be inaccurate. While a model can never perfectly represent an actual system, they are useful for simplifying a system to allow for better understanding of its behavior. Scientific laws are statements of natural behavior that have stood the test of time and have been found to produce accurate and repeatable results in all testing. A theory is a statement of behavior that consolidates all current observations. Theories are similar to laws in that they describe natural behavior, but are more recently developed and, as such, are more susceptible to being proved wrong. Theories may eventually become laws if they stand up to repeated scrutiny and testing over the course of many years.

Overarching concepts

There are several concepts that transcend the various branches of science and can be found as integral parts of physics, chemistry, biology, and other areas of study. One of these concepts is the system. A system is an arbitrarily sized group of entities that are taken to be a single unit. Systems may consist of physical bodies or of abstract concepts that intertwine. Systems will often be modeled by either mathematical expressions or physical-scale models, depending on the type of system and the purpose of the scale. In scale models, it is important to keep in mind that scale can have a huge effect on the behavior of a system. This can be clearly seen in models of the solar system. The gravitational effects in a room-sized solar system model will be entirely negligible due to its reduced size. Other phenomena, such as nuclear attractive forces, will only be observed on the atomic level. If the state of a system is constant, it is at equilibrium. Equilibrium may be either static or dynamic. For example, a pair of side-by-side pools are in static equilibrium if there is no water being transferred between them. They are in dynamic equilibrium if equal amounts of water are being transferred between the pools in each direction. In the design of physical components, something that may be encountered is the interrelationship between form and function. If one of these two goals takes priority, that one will dictate the other. For instance, if the external appearance of a building is considered to be of higher importance than its utility, the functionality of the building may be limited.

Scientific measurement and unit systems

The basis of quantitative measurement is the unit system. In order to properly describe how large, how heavy, or how hot something is, it is necessary to have some reference unit. The most commonly used unit system in the world is the SI, short for the Systeme International d'Unites, although the English system is still in popular use in the United States. In SI, there are base units and derived units. Derived units may be stated as some combination of the base units. The SI base units for length, mass, time, temperature, and electric current are meter (m), kilogram (kg), second (s), kelvin (K), and ampere (A), respectively. Some common derived units are newtons ($kg\text{-}m/s^2$) and pascals ($kg/m\text{-}s^2$). Most SI units can be scaled up or down by adding a prefix. To alter a unit by 10^3, 10^6, or 10^9, add a prefix of kilo (k), mega (M), or giga (G). For instance, a kilometer (km) is 10^3 meters. To change the unit by a factor of 10^{-3}, 10^{-6}, or 10^{-9}, add a prefix of milli (m), micro (μ), or nano (n). For instance, a microsecond (μs) is 10^{-6} seconds. It is important to note that the SI base unit kilogram has already employed a prefix to scale up the smaller unit, gram (g). Order of magnitude is a concept that deals with comparison between two values. If one value differs from the other by a factor of 10^n, it may be said that it differs by n orders of magnitude.

Other SI base units include the mole and the candela. Some lesser used prefixes include: hecto (h), 10^2; deca (da), 10^1; deci (d), 10^{-1}; and centi (c), 10^{-2}.

Scientific knowledge

Perhaps the greatest peculiarity of scientific knowledge is that, at the same time that it is taken as fact, it may be disproved. Current scientific knowledge is the basis from which new discoveries are made. Yet even knowledge that has stood for hundreds of years is not considered too infallible to be challenged. If someone can create an experiment whose results consistently and reproducibly defy a law that has been in place for generations, that law will be nullified. It is absolutely essential, however, that these reproductions of the experiment be conducted by many different scientists who are in isolation from one another so there is no bias or interacting effects on the results.

Interpretation of tables, charts, and graphs

One of the reasons data are so often plotted on graphs is that this format makes it much easier to see trends and draw conclusions. For instance, on a simple position vs. time graph, the slope of the curve indicates the object's velocity at each point in time. If the curve becomes level, this means the object is not moving. In a simple velocity vs. time graph, the slope of the curve indicates the object's acceleration at each point in time. Additionally, the area contained under the curve indicates the total distance traveled. For instance, if the object is traveling at a constant 5 m/s for 10 s, the velocity vs. time graph will be a straight line at y = 5 between x = 0 and x = 10. The area under this curve is (5 m/s)(10 s) = 50 m. Thus, the object traveled 50 meters.

Nearly any type of quantity may be graphed, so it is important to always check the axis labels to ensure that you know what the graph represents and what units are being used.

Data collection and analysis

In order to take data measurements from their experimental setups, scientists will often use measurement devices wired to a computer running data-acquisition software. This allows them to take numerous readings per second if necessary. Once the data is collected, it will often be organized using a spreadsheet, such as Microsoft Excel. This multipurpose program contains several options for displaying the data in graphs or charts, as well as tools for performing statistical analyses or linear regressions. Linear regression is a technique used to determine whether gathered data fits a particular trend or equation. It attempts to fit a common line or curve equation to the data set. A very important concept to understand when taking data is that of significant figures. Significant figures, or significant digits, indicate how precisely a quantity is known. Each non-zero digit is always significant. A zero is significant if either: 1) it is to the right of both a non-zero digit and the decimal point; or 2) it is between two other significant digits. For instance, 1.0230 has five significant figures while 0.0230 has only three because the trailing zero is the only zero to the right of both a non-zero and the decimal. When multiplying (or dividing), the product (quotient) has as many significant figures as the factor (dividend or divisor) with the fewest. When adding (or subtracting), the sum (difference) should be rounded to the highest final decimal place of the involved terms.

(3.4 + 56.78 = 60.18 --> 60.2, three significant figures)

Data errors and error analysis

No measurements are ever 100% accurate. There is always some amount of error regardless of how careful the observer or how good his equipment. The important thing for the scientist to know is how much error is present in a given measurement. Two commonly misunderstood terms regarding error are accuracy and precision. Accuracy is a measure of how close a measurement is to the true value. Precision is a measure of how close repeated measurements are to one another. Error is usually quantified using a confidence interval and an uncertainty value. For instance, if the quantity is measured as 100 ± 2 on a 95% confidence interval, this means that there is a 95% chance that the actual value falls between 98 and 102.

When looking for the uncertainty in a derived quantity such as density, the errors in the constituent quantities, mass and volume in this case, are propagated to the derived quantity. The percent uncertainty in the density, U_ρ/ρ, can be found by the equation: $U_\rho/\rho = sqrt((U_m/m)^2 + (U_V/V)^2)$.

Basic safety procedures

The most important safety precaution is to be prepared. Be acquainted with all potential hazards of any procedure, as well as all equipment, its associated safety procedures, and all lab manuals before beginning an experiment. Calibrate all equipment properly and handle it with care and only for its intended purpose. Read all material safety data sheets before beginning a procedure. Perform all procedures yourself before assigning them to students.

Secure and label all biological, chemical, and carcinogenic materials, away from heat and food, not on a high surface or on the floor, and segregated by reactivity. Follow all local disposal procedures for used lab materials, labeling all chemical and biological waste. Make sure all storage and waste containers are leakproof. Avoid contamination. Use distilled water in the lab, not tap water, as tap water contains impurities. Clean and rinse all glassware after use. Secure items with clamps as necessary. Use, and have students use, goggles, gloves, and lab coats. Take extra caution with knives, glass rods, weights, and any potentially injurious materials.

Heat

Periodically check the gas connections and burners in the laboratory. Unless the gas is actively being used, keep the master gas valve off at all times. Never heat anything in a closed container, where pressure can build, and use only glassware approved for lab use. Use gloves, goggles, and fire-retardant pads as needed around hot materials. Never place a heat source in a location where it can be knocked over accidentally. Keep all flames and gas water heaters far from the vapors of flammable liquids.

Pressure

When using a pressure cooker, never exceed 20 pounds per square inch of pressure. Never open a hot pressure cooker. Always make sure the safety valve is in working order.

Electrical

Know the location of the main cutoff switch for the laboratory. Regularly check all electrical connections, live wires, and batteries before turning the power on. All outlets should be GFCI, and extension cords should only be used extremely judiciously.

Keep all electrical current away from flammable materials and water. Use only 6- or 12-volt direct current, and double-insulate or ground all power equipment.

In all procedures, the insertion of the plug should be the last step in setup; when disassembling, remove the plug first. Use only one hand in all procedures involving an electrical current. Never allow oneself or a student to become part of an electrical circuit.

Sound

Never exceed 110 decibels, which causes hearing damage. When using a high-speed siren disk, make sure to use the safety disk.

Radiation

Shield all people properly when using X-rays, and keep them at least 10 feet from any radiation experiment. Periodically check all tubes, including vacuum, heat effect, magnetic, and deflection tubes. Enclose cathode rays in a frame, never allow students to use them themselves, and operate them for the shortest possible time and at the lowest practical voltage.

Radioactivity

Ensure you have access to a radiation survey meter before doing any radioactivity experiment, and make sure you have been trained properly in equipment handling, demonstration, and disposal procedures. Never use bare hands to handle radioactive materials. Shield all people from all radioactive material as required, by paper, glass, or lead. Store all radioactive material securely, and dispose of it properly.

Light

Do not use broken mirrors, prisms, or glass; grind or tape those with sharp edges. Periodically check all connections for spectroscopic light voltage. Shield all people from ultraviolet and infrared light sources. Be aware of students with neurological conditions (for instance, epilepsy) that make them susceptible to strobe lights. Never allow students to look directly into the sun; design viewfinders for solar-eclipse viewing.

Lasers

Be aware of the laser classification system, and know which type you are using. Shield all people from direct exposure to a laser; contain people's movements when using lasers to avoid inadvertent exposure. Project lasers only onto non-reflective surfaces, maintain a sufficient light level to prevent pupil dilation, and make sure to shield all prisms and reflective objects. Use the minimum effective optical power. Terminate the beam at a point beyond the furthest point of interest, in a non-reflective material. Be familiar with the safety features of a laser projector, and use beam stops when the laser is not actively being used. Equip the laser with a key switch if possible.

Basic safety rules

It is critical to plan for all eventualities when it comes to laboratory safety. Maintain all safety equipment and know how to use it. Understand first-aid procedures and re-familiarize yourself with the relevant ones when planning student experiments.

Distribute safety rules to students, and keep instructions for all safety procedures readily available for all parties. Post multiple and clear signs warning of any dangers associated with hazardous chemicals or delicate equipment. Post copies of all laboratory rules and spell out appropriate material-handling procedures.

Be prepared and willing to seek help in the event of an emergency. Students should never clean chemical or biological spills; only the teacher should, using appropriate chemical spill kits or bleach as appropriate. Large spills must be reported to the school administration and the fire department as soon as possible. You must also immediately report any injuries or accidents to the school administration and a health provider.

Students must wear safety goggles during heating, dissecting, and using acids and bases. Long hair should be tied back, and hands washed before and after experiments. Food must be forbidden in the lab.

Setting up a science laboratory

The most important safety guideline in setting up a laboratory is to plan well and become familiar with all equipment and materials. Understand theoretically as well as practically the risks and effects of all materials you are using; know how to neutralize the effects of all materials. Set up all equipment so that it is in no danger of falling. Verify the locations and functionality of all safety equipment. Regularly monitor the condition and stock of all materials, including safety materials. Always choose the least hazardous effective materials for all procedures.

Perform all experiments yourself before doing them with students. Provide clear instructions on all procedures, including waste-disposal procedures, to students before having them perform them. Reinforce students' knowledge of safety procedures throughout the term.

Keep the laboratory locked at all times when not in use.

Legal Responsibilities

At all levels of the legal system, it is the responsibility of a teacher to provide a safe environment for students. Never leave the room accessible to unsupervised students; if you must leave the room, provide students with proper alternative supervision. Familiarize students with safety procedures, and review them regularly. Posting the rules is insufficient; you must continually review them with students. If a procedure cannot be safely carried out, it must not be performed.

Avoid negligence. Always consider all possible outcomes before performing a procedure, and exercise care to minimize any danger to students and property. State Departments of Education have encoded the specific legal responsibilities of science teachers; familiarize yourself with state laws.

Basic safety equipment

All labs should contain the following items:
- Bucket of sand for absorption of spills and smothering of alkali fires
- Fire blanket
- First-aid kit, containing bandages and antiseptic
- One GFCI within two feet of all water supplies
- Exit signs
- Emergency shower
- Emergency eyewash station
- Splashproof eye protection for all parties, and a means to sanitize it
- Face shields
- Emergency exhaust fans that vent to the outside of the building
- Fire blanket
- Gloves, both rubber and nitrile
- Master cutoff switches for gas, electricity, and compressed air
- ABC fire extinguisher
- Storage cabinets for flammable items
- Chemical spill-control kit
- Fume hood with a spark-proof motor
- Flame-retardant lab aprons
- Mercury clean-up kit
- Neutralizing agents, including acetic acid and sodium bicarbonate
- Signs drawing attention to potential hazards
- Segregated, clearly labeled containers for storing broken glassware, flammable items, solid chemicals, corrosive items, and waste.

Major energy issues

Since the Industrial Revolution, energy for industrialized human needs has come from fossil fuels, particularly coal and petroleum, but increased use means that this source of fuel is quickly being depleted, in addition to causing pollution. The search for alternative, safe sources of energy for an increasingly industrialized world population is therefore increasingly important to scientists.

An ideal source of energy would be efficient, renewable, and sustainable. Various sources of alternative energy have been proposed, including wind, water, solar, nuclear, geothermal, and biomass, but thus far none have been made practically available on a large scale. Some, such as wind and water, blight the landscape, while the conversion methods for other sources, such as solar and biomass, are still relatively inefficient. The scientific community is still unclear on the best way to harness the power of photosynthesis and biomass for energy needs in a way that would allow a large-scale energy industry to use it. Scientists remain at work studying the long-term solutions to an increasingly urgent problem for humanity.

Effects of improvements in scientific and technological knowledge

Since the Industrial Revolution, technological improvements to agricultural production have made agriculture productive on an industrial scale, while advances in medical knowledge have brought about the cures for many diseases. People in many parts of the world live longer and enjoy a higher standard of living than ever before.

However, this progress does not come without a price. The effects on the environment of industrialization are almost exclusively negative. Monoculture farming practices resulting from industrialization mean that farming no longer exists as a closed ecosystem; the chemical fertilizers that create record crop yields have changed the nutrient environment, and the waste products of industrial agriculture pollute the water rather than fertilizing the soil. Increased travel creates dangerous carbon dioxide emissions and depletes the earth's limited store of fossil fuels. Water pollution means limited access to potable water, and deforestation has begun to change the makeup of ecosystems and cause the extinction of many species. Through the increased contact made available by improved technology, however, humans are also collaborating on solutions to these new problems.

Increased production of consumer goods

Electric-based, industrial production of manufactured goods has led to an increase in the standard of living for many, especially those in the industrialized world. Consumer goods are produced more cheaply than ever before, since the means of production is not as dependent on the physical abilities of human beings. Scientific advancements have led to a huge number of new synthetic materials from which goods can be made, including plastics and nylon.

However, this increased production damages the environment. Waste products are now created of which humans can make no use, a new phenomenon. Trash created from these new products is buried in landfills, where it has no access to the air, water, and sunlight that are a necessary part of biodegradation; trash made from some synthetic materials does not biodegrade at all. While some waste products can be recycled, many byproducts of industrial manufacturing are hazardous, with no safe way to dispose of them. The long-term sustainability of the environment as a result of massively increased consumer production is an issue of increasing urgency for scientists.

Nuclear power controversy

Nuclear fission power, while sustainable, has a host of attendant controversial problems. Among them is the incredibly dangerous transportation and long-term storage of its radioactive waste products, for which there is still no safe long-term solution. Its effects on those environments and creatures that come in contact with nuclear waste are still largely unknown. In addition, nuclear materials can be used in weaponry, and accidents at nuclear power plants like the one at Chernobyl can be devastating for thousands of years.

Scientists continue their study of the process of nuclear fusion, hoping that if humans can learn to harness the energy produced by smashing atoms rather than splitting them, the attendant problems of nuclear waste storage will be minimized.

Management of non-renewable resources

Non-renewable resources include minerals, which are created naturally over millions of years. The industrialized world extracts minerals for fuel as well as for use in electronic equipment and medicine. Increased human extraction of non-renewable resources has endangered their availability, and over-mining has created other ecological problems, including runoff and water pollution. The use of fossil fuels for energy and transportation causes air pollution and is unsustainable. Fossil fuels cannot be replaced once depleted, and they are being depleted at an increasing rate. The need to find a sustainable alternative to the use of non-renewable fossil fuels is imperative.

Management of renewable resources

Natural resources can be divided into two types, renewable and non-renewable. Renewable resources include plants and animals, along with water, air, and soil.

A pre-industrial earth was a self-sustaining system, maintaining a natural balance among plants, animals, and non-living elements in which waste products from one natural process were the fuel for another. Modern humans have intervened in this process in a way that upsets the natural balance of life. Humans have introduced non-native species from one part of the world to another, resulting in the devastation of local populations. Industrial-scale buildings can create disasters for local ecosystems, ruining habitats for animal populations.

Humans remove an increasing amount of the world's resources for industrial use, too quickly for nature to recover from easily. Renewable resources must be carefully managed to maintain a balanced ecosystem; over-harvesting of forests or over-hunting of animal populations can be devastating. Pollution of the air and water with chemical pollutants has far-reaching effects on the ecosystems of the earth, including the depletion of the ozone layer that protects earth life from ultraviolet rays, as does the removal of forests that produce the earth's oxygen.

Social impacts of science and technology

Recent developments in science and technology have had both positive and negative effects on human society. The issue of sustainable growth is an increasingly important one, as humans realize that the resources they use are not unlimited. Genetic research into diseases, stem cell research, and cloning technology have created great controversies as they have been introduced, and an increasing number of people reject the morality of scientific practices like animal testing in the pursuit of scientific advancement. In addition, an increasingly technology-based world has produced a new social inequality based on access to computers and Internet technology.

These issues are beginning to be debated at all levels of human government, from city councils to the United Nations. Does science provide the authoritative answer to all human problems, or do ethics carry weight in scientific debates as well? Ultimately, humans must weigh the competing needs of facilitating scientific pursuits and maintaining an ethical society as they face new technological questions.

Recent applications of science and technology

Scientific and technological developments have led to the widespread availability of technologies heretofore unheard of, including cellular phones, satellite-based applications, and a worldwide network of connected computers. Some of the notable recent applications include:

Health care: Antibiotics, genetic screening for diseases, the sequencing of the human genome. Issues include problems with health care distribution on an increasingly industrialized planet.

The environment: Computerized models of climate change and pollution monitoring. Issues include increased pollution of the water, air, and soil, and the over-harvesting of natural resources with mechanized equipment.

Agriculture: Genetic improvements in agricultural practices, including increased output on the same amount of arable land. Issues include unknown environmental effects of hybrid species, cross-pollination with organic species, and pollution caused by synthetic chemical fertilizers.
Information technology: New Internet-based industries, increased worldwide collaboration, and access to information. Issues include the depletion of natural resources for electronics production.

Contributing individuals to physics

Archimedes (ancient Greece)
Archimedes designed the compound pulley, articulated the principles of the lever, and made important contributions to engineering and geometry, calculating the area of a sphere and an ellipse and approximating the value of pi. Archimedes' Law of the Lever states that when objects are set at distances reciprocally proportional to their respective weights, they are in equilibrium.

Amedeo Avogadro (Italian, 18th century)

Avogadro established the principles of molarity, clarified the relationship between atoms and molecules, and formalized what became known as Avogadro's principle: that equal volumes of gases held at the same pressure and temperature will contain an equal number of molecules, and that their masses will be proportionate to their respective molecular weights. Avogadro's constant is the number of particles present in 1 mole of any substance.

Robert Boyle (Irish, 17th century)

Though regarded as the first modern chemist, Boyle also distinguished himself in physics and contributed to experimental design. Boyle's Law is a mathematical expression of the relationship between volume and pressure within an ideal gas.

Sir Isaac Newton (English, 17th/18th century)

Newton, one of the most important scientists of all time, made critical breakthroughs in the understanding of scientific methods, motion, and optics. Newton described universal gravitation, observed that white light contains the entire spectrum of colors, and discovered the calculus independently of Leibniz (who is credited with it). The three Newtonian laws of motion are:

- An object in motion (or at rest) remains in motion (or at rest) unless acted upon by an external force.
- Force equals mass times acceleration.
- For every action, there is an equal and opposite reaction.

Galileo Galilei (Italian, 17th century)

Galileo determined that all bodies, regardless of mass, fall at the same rate. He argued that motion is continuous, changed only when an external force is applied to it (later incorporated in Newton's laws of motion). His work in astronomy was important in confirming Copernicus' heliocentric model of the solar system. His principle of relativity states that the laws of physics are constant within a constantly moving system, a theory that became central to Einstein's work on relativity.

Marie Curie (Polish/French, 19th century)

Curie was the foremost pioneer of radioactivity. She isolated the radioactive elements polonium and radium, and established that radioactivity was a property of an atom itself rather than of the relationship between multiple molecules.

Michael Faraday (English, 18th/19th century)

Faraday's most important work was in the fields of electromagnetism and electrochemistry. His work led directly to some of the most important breakthroughs in electrical technology of the twentieth century. Faraday introduced the concept of fields to the study of magnetism and electricity. He discovered what would become known as the Faraday Effect, the effect of a strong magnetic field on the behavior of light rays. The Farad (the SI unit of capacitance) and the Faraday constant (the amount of charge on one mole of electrons) are both named for him.

Wilhelm Ostwald (Latvian, 19th/20th century)

One of the founders of classical physical chemistry, Ostwald did important work on the properties of atomic particles, and defined a mole as the molecular weight, in grams, of a given substance.

Albert Einstein (German, 20th century)

Einstein, the most famous twentieth-century scientist, was a theoretical physicist whose special theory of relativity describes the relationship of time and space, and mass and gravity. In it, he declared that gravity is a consequence of the properties of space-time and that the speed of light is constant. He hypothesized that electromagnetic energy can be absorbed or expelled by matter in quanta, and discovered the photoelectric effect.

Stephen Hawking (English, 20th/21st century)

Hawking's principal fields of research are theoretical cosmology and quantum gravity. Expanding on Einstein's work, he has hypothesized about the physical properties of black holes, described conditions necessary for a singularity, and made important contributions in string theory, in an attempt to generalize Einstein's special theory of relativity.

J. Robert Oppenheimer (American, 20th century)

Oppenheimer's scientific contributions are in astrophysics, nuclear physics, and quantum field theory. He served as scientific director of the Manhattan Project, which constructed the first atomic bomb.

Linus Pauling (American, 20th century)

Pauling applied new discoveries in quantum mechanics to the field of chemistry, pioneering the study of molecular medicine. He researched the biochemical origins of genetic diseases like sickle-cell anemia.

Enrico Fermi (Italian/American, 20th century)

Fermi discovered the process of making elements artificially radioactive by bombarding them with neutrons. He divided elements into the two groups of fermions and bosons. His work on nuclear reactions led him to participate in the Manhattan Project.

Niels Bohr (Danish, 20th century)

Bohr established that the number of electrons determined the atom's chemical properties. He articulated the organization of electrons, in discrete orbits around an atom's nucleus, and that electrons could move orbits, thereby emitting radiation—the basis for quantum theory. Bohr worked on the Manhattan Project along with Oppenheimer and Fermi.

Physical Science

Atoms

All matter consists of atoms. Atoms consist of a nucleus and electrons. The nucleus consists of protons and neutrons. The properties of these are measurable; they have mass and an electrical charge. The nucleus is positively charged due to the presence of protons. Electrons are negatively charged and orbit the nucleus. The nucleus has considerably more mass than the surrounding electrons. Atoms can bond together to make molecules. Atoms that have an equal number of protons and electrons are electrically neutral. If the number of protons and electrons in an atom is not equal, the atom has a positive or negative charge and is an ion.

Atoms are extremely small. A hydrogen atom is about 5×10^{-8} mm in diameter. According to some estimates, five trillion hydrogen atoms could fit on the head of a pin. Atomic radius refers to the average distance between the nucleus and the outermost electron. Models of atoms that include the proton, nucleus, and electrons typically show the electrons very close to the nucleus and revolving around it, similar to how the Earth orbits the sun. However, another model relates the Earth as the nucleus and its atmosphere as electrons, which is the basis of the term "electron cloud." Another description is that electrons swarm around the nucleus. It should be noted that these atomic models are not to scale. A more accurate representation would be a nucleus with a diameter of about 2 cm in a stadium. The electrons would be in the bleachers. This model is similar to the not-to-scale solar system model.

Matter refers to substances that have mass and occupy space (or volume). The traditional definition of matter describes it as having three states: solid, liquid, and gas. These different states are caused by differences in the distances and angles between molecules or atoms, which result in differences in the energy that binds them. Solid structures are rigid or nearly rigid and have strong bonds. Molecules or atoms of liquids move around and have weak bonds, although they are not weak enough to readily break. Molecules or atoms of gases move almost independently of each other, are typically far apart, and do not form bonds. The current definition of matter describes it as having four states. The fourth is plasma, which is an ionized gas that has some electrons that are described as free because they are not bound to an atom or molecule.

An atom is one of the most basic units of matter. An atom consists of a central nucleus surrounded by electrons. The nucleus of an atom consists of protons and neutrons. It is positively charged, dense, and heavier than the surrounding electrons. The plural form of nucleus is nuclei. Neutrons are the uncharged atomic particles contained within the nucleus. The number of neutrons in a nucleus can be represented as "N." Along with neutrons, protons make up the nucleus of an atom. The number of protons in the nucleus determines the atomic number of an element. Carbon atoms, for example, have six protons. The atomic number of carbon is 6. Nucleon refers collectively to neutrons and protons. Electrons are atomic particles that are negatively charged and orbit the nucleus of an atom. The number of protons minus the number of electrons indicates the charge of an atom.

The atomic number of an element refers to the number of protons in the nucleus of an atom. It is a unique identifier. It can be represented as Z. Atoms with a neutral charge have an atomic number that is equal to the number of electrons. Atomic mass is also known as the mass number. The atomic mass is the total number of protons and neutrons in the nucleus of an atom. It is referred to as "A." The atomic mass (A) is equal to the number of protons (Z) plus the number of neutrons (N). This can be represented by the equation $A = Z + N$. The mass of electrons in an atom is basically insignificant because it is so small. Atomic weight may sometimes be referred to as "relative atomic mass," but should not be confused with atomic mass. Atomic weight is the ratio of the average mass per atom of a sample (which can include various isotopes of an element) to 1/12 of the mass of an atom of carbon-12.

An element is matter with one particular type of atom. It can be identified by its atomic number, or the number of protons in its nucleus. There are approximately 117 elements currently known, 94 of which occur naturally on Earth. Elements from the periodic table include hydrogen, carbon, iron, helium, mercury, and oxygen. Atoms combine to form molecules. For example, two atoms of hydrogen (H) and one atom of oxygen (O) combine to form water (H_2O).

Compounds are substances containing two or more elements. Compounds are formed by chemical reactions and frequently have different properties than the original elements. Compounds are decomposed by a chemical reaction rather than separated by a physical one.

Binary compounds refer to compounds that contain only two elements. They can be ionic or covalent. Binary ionic compounds are formed by cations (metallic positive ions) and anions (nonmetal negative ions). Ionic compounds are not molecules. The suffix "ide" is used if there is one anion, as in the case of cuprous oxide, for example. Another example is that fluorine is an element, while fluoride is the negative ion of fluorine. The binary compound barium fluoride would be written as BaF_2. This is because one barium ion has a charge of +2 and one fluoride ion has a charge of -1, so it would take two fluoride ions to balance out the one barium ion. If there is no charge symbol, it is assumed that the charge is 1. The suffixes "ate" or "ite" are used when there is more than one anion, as in the case of mercurous nitrate, for example. A ternary compound is one formed of three elements.

Hydrogen bonds are weaker than covalent and ionic bonds, and refer to the type of attraction in an electronegative atom such as oxygen, fluorine, or nitrogen. Hydrogen bonds can form within a single molecule or between molecules. A water molecule is polar, meaning it is partially positively charged on one end (the hydrogen end) and partially negatively charged on the other (the oxygen end). This is because the hydrogen atoms are arranged around the oxygen atom in a close tetrahedron. Hydrogen is oxidized (its number of electrons is reduced) when it bonds with oxygen to form water. Hydrogen bonds tend not only to be weak, but also short-lived. They also tend to be numerous. Hydrogen bonds give water many of its important properties, including its high specific heat and high heat of vaporization, its solvent qualities, its adhesiveness and cohesiveness, its hydrophobic qualities, and its ability to float in its solid form. Hydrogen bonds are also an important component of proteins, nucleic acids, and DNA.

Elements are represented in upper case letters. If there is no subscript, it indicates there is only one atom of the element. Otherwise, the subscript indicates the number of atoms. In molecular formulas, elements are organized according to the Hill system. Carbon is first, hydrogen comes next, and the remaining elements are listed in alphabetical order. If there is no carbon, all elements are listed alphabetically. There are a couple of exceptions to these rules. First, oxygen is usually listed last in oxides. Second, in ionic compounds the positive ion is listed first, followed by the negative ion. In CO_2, for example, C indicates 1 atom of carbon and O_2 indicates 2 atoms of oxygen. The compound is carbon dioxide. The formula for ammonia (an ionic compound) is NH_3, which is one atom of nitrogen and three of hydrogen. H_2O is two atoms of hydrogen and one of oxygen. Sugar is $C_6H_{12}O_6$, which is 6 atoms of carbon, 12 of hydrogen, and 6 of oxygen.

Chemical properties are qualities of a substance which can't be determined by simply looking at the substance and must be determined through chemical reactions. Some chemical properties of elements include: atomic number, electron configuration, electrons per shell, electronegativity, atomic radius, and isotopes.

In contrast to chemical properties, physical properties can be observed or measured without chemical reactions. These include properties such as color, elasticity, mass, volume, and temperature. Mass is a measure of the amount of substance in an object. Weight is a measure of the gravitational pull of Earth on an object. Volume is a measure of the amount of space occupied. There are many formulas to determine volume. For example, the volume of a cube is the length of one side cubed (a^3) and the volume of a rectangular prism is length times width times height ($l \cdot w \cdot h$). The volume of an irregular shape can be determined by how much water it displaces. Density is a measure of the amount of mass per unit volume. The formula to find density is mass divided by volume ($D=m/V$). It is expressed in terms of mass per cubic unit, such as grams per cubic centimeter (g/cm^3). Specific gravity is a measure of the ratio of a substance's density compared to the density of water.

Both physical changes and chemical reactions are everyday occurrences. Physical changes do not result in different substances. For example, when water becomes ice it has undergone a physical change, but not a chemical change. It has changed its form, but not its composition. It is still H_2O. Chemical properties are concerned with the constituent particles that make up the physicality of a substance. Chemical properties are apparent when chemical changes occur. The chemical properties of a substance are influenced by its electron configuration, which is determined in part by the number of protons in the nucleus (the atomic number). Carbon, for example, has 6 protons and 6 electrons. It is an element's outermost valence electrons that mainly determine its chemical properties. Chemical reactions may release or consume energy.

Solutions and Mixtures

A solution is a homogeneous mixture. A mixture is two or more different substances that are mixed together, but not combined chemically. Homogeneous mixtures are those that are uniform in their composition. Solutions consist of a solute (the substance that is dissolved) and a solvent (the substance that does the dissolving). An example is sugar water. The solvent is the water and the solute is the sugar. The intermolecular attraction between the solvent and the solute is called solvation. Hydration refers to solutions in which water is the solvent. Solutions are formed when the forces of the molecules of the solute and the solvent are as strong as the individual molecular forces of the solute and the solvent. An example is that salt (NaCl) dissolves in water to create a solution. The Na^+ and the Cl^- ions in salt interact with the molecules of water and vice versa to overcome the individual molecular forces of the solute and the solvent.

The term dilute is used when there is less solute. Adding more solvent is known as diluting a solution, as is removing a portion of the solute. Concentrated is the term used when there is more solute. Adding more solute makes a solution more concentrated, as does removing a portion of the solvent.

For solvation to occur, bonds of similar strength must be broken and formed. Nonpolar substances are usually soluble in nonpolar solvents. Ionic and polar matter is usually soluble in polar solvents. Water is a polar solvent. Oil is nonpolar. Heptane (C_7H_{16}) is another nonpolar liquid that is said to be immiscible in water, meaning it can't combine with water. The hydrogen bonds of the water molecules are stronger than the London dispersion forces of the heptane. Polar molecules such as NH_3 (ammonia), SO_2 (sulfur dioxide), and H_2S (hydrogen sulfide) are termed hydrophilic, meaning they readily combine with water. Nonpolar molecules, including the noble gases and other gases such as He (helium), Ne (neon), and CO_2 (carbon dioxide) are termed hydrophobic, meaning they repel or do not readily combine with water. One way to remember this is that "like dissolves like." Polar solvents dissolve polar solutes, while nonpolar solvents dissolve nonpolar solutes.

Solids tend to dissolve faster when the temperature is increased. Higher temperatures help break bonds through an increase in kinetic energy. Solubility tends to increase for solids being dissolved in water as the temperature approaches 100 °C, but at higher temperatures ionic solutes tend to become less soluble. Gases tend to be less soluble at higher temperatures. When solutions are saturated at high temperatures, the solute will precipitate (return to solid form) and "fall out of the solution" as the solution cools. Melting points can be lowered by using a solvent such as salt on icy roads, which lowers the freezing point of ice. Adding salt to water when making ice cream also lowers the melting point of the water. A solution's melting point is usually lower than the melting point of the solvent alone. Pressure has little effect on the solubility of liquid solutions. In gas solutions, an increase in pressure increases solubility, and vice versa.

The concentration of a solution is measured in terms of molarity. One molar (M) is equal to a quantity of moles of solute per liter of solution. Adding one mole of a substance to one liter of solution would most likely result in a molarity greater than one. The amount of substance should be measured into a small amount of solution, and then more solution should be added to reach a volume of one liter to ensure accuracy. Molality refers to the concentration or ratio of moles of solute per kilogram of solvent. Colligative properties refer to how a solvent acts when it becomes a solution. Colligative properties are determined by the number of solute molecules rather than their exact characteristics. Some examples of colligative properties are that a solution's osmotic pressure and boiling point increase and its melting point decreases when the amount of solute is increased. As the amount of solute is increased, vapor will decrease above the solution when it is composed of a solid, nonvolatile solute dissolved in a liquid.

Atomic Theory

Atomic theory is concerned with the characteristics and properties of atoms that make up matter. It deals with matter on a microscopic level as opposed to a macroscopic level. Atomic theory, for instance, discusses the kinetic motion of atoms in order to explain the properties of macroscopic quantities of matter. John Dalton (1766-1844) is credited with making many contributions to the field of atomic theory that are still considered valid. This includes the notion that all matter consists of atoms and that atoms are indestructible. In other words, atoms can be neither created nor destroyed. This is also the theory behind the conservation of matter, which explains why chemical reactions do not result in any detectable gains or losses in matter. This holds true for chemical reactions and smaller scale processes. When dealing with large amounts of energy, however, atoms can be destroyed by nuclear reactions. This can happen in particle colliders or atom smashers.

There have been many revisions to theories regarding the structure of atoms and their particles. Part of the challenge in developing an understanding of matter is that atoms and their particles are too small to be seen. It is believed that the first conceptualization of the atom was developed by Democritus in 400 B.C. Some of the more notable models are the solid sphere or billiard ball model postulated by John Dalton, the plum pudding or raisin bun model by J.J. Thomson, the planetary or nuclear model by Ernest Rutherford, the Bohr or orbit model by Niels Bohr, and the electron cloud or quantum mechanical model by Louis de Broglie and Erwin Schrodinger. Rutherford directed the alpha scattering experiment that discounted the plum pudding model. The shortcoming of the Bohr model was the belief that electrons orbited in fixed rather than changing ecliptic orbits.

Radioactivity

Radioisotopes, also known as radionuclides or radioactive isotopes, are atoms that have an unstable nucleus. This is a nucleus that has excess energy and the potential to make radiation particles within the nucleus (subatomic particles) or undergo radioactive decay, which can result in the emission of gamma rays. Radionuclides may occur naturally, but can also be artificially produced.

Radioactive decay occurs when an unstable atomic nucleus spontaneously loses energy by emitting ionizing particles and radiation. Decay is a form of energy transfer, as energy is lost. It also results in different products. Before decay there is one type of atom, called the parent nuclide. After decay there are one or more different products, called the daughter nuclide(s). Radioactivity refers to particles that are emitted from nuclei as a result of nuclear instability.

Radioactive half-life is the time it takes for half of the radioactive nuclei in a sample to undergo radioactive decay. Radioactive decay rates are usually expressed in terms of half-lives. The different types of radioactivity lead to different decay paths, which transmute the nuclei into other chemical elements. Decay products (or daughter nuclides) make radioactive dating possible. Decay chains are a series of decays that result in different products. For example, uranium-238 is often found in granite. Its decay chain includes 14 daughter products. It eventually becomes a stable isotope of lead, which is why lead is often found with deposits of uranium ore. Its first half-life is equivalent to the approximate age of the earth, about 4.5 billion years. One of its products is radon, a radioactive gas. Radiation is when energy is emitted by one body and absorbed by another. Nuclear weapons, nuclear reactors, and radioactive substances are all examples of things that involve ionizing radiation. Acoustic and electromagnetic radiation are other types of radiation.

Isotopes that have not been observed to decay are stable, or non-radioactive, isotopes. It is not known whether some stable isotopes may have such long decay times that observing decay is not possible. Currently, 80 elements have one or more stable isotopes. There are 256 known stable isotopes in total. Carbon, for example, has three isotopes. Two (carbon-12 and carbon-13) are stable and one (carbon-14) is radioactive. Radioactive isotopes have unstable nuclei and can undergo spontaneous nuclear reactions, which results in particles or radiation being emitted. It cannot be predicted when a specific nucleus will decay, but large groups of identical nuclei decay at predictable rates. Knowledge about rates of decay can be used to estimate the age of materials that contain radioactive isotopes.

The conservation of mass number is a concept related to nuclear reactions. Two conditions are required to balance a nuclear reaction. They are conservation of mass number and conservation of nuclear charge. In a nuclear equation, the mass numbers should be equal on each side of the arrow. In this type of equation, the mass number is in superscript in front of the element and the atomic number is in subscript. The total number of nucleons is the same even though the product elements are different. For example, when a specific isotope of uranium decays into thorium and helium, the original mass number of uranium is 238. After the reaction, the mass number of thorium is 234 and the mass number of helium is 4 (238 = 234 + 4). The mass number is the same on both sides of the equation.

Ionizing radiation is that which can cause an electron to detach from an atom. It occurs in radioactive reactions and comes in three types: alpha (α), beta (β), and gamma (γ). Alpha rays are positive, beta rays are negative, and gamma rays are neutral. Alpha particles are larger than beta particles and can cause severe damage if ingested. Because of their large mass, however, they can be stopped easily. Even paper can protect against this type of radiation. Beta particles can be beta-minus or beta-plus. Beta-minus particles contain an energetic electron, while beta-plus particles are emitted by positrons and can result in gamma photons. Beta particles can be stopped with thin metal. Gamma rays are a type of high energy electromagnetic radiation consisting of photons. Gamma radiation rids the decaying nucleus of excess energy after it has emitted either alpha or beta radiation. Gamma rays can cause serious damage when absorbed by living tissue, and it takes thick lead to stop them. Alpha, beta, and gamma radiation can also have positive applications.

Nuclear fission and nuclear fusion are similar in that they occur in the nucleus of an atom, can release great amounts of energy, and result in the formation of different elements (known as nuclear transmutation). They are different in that one breaks apart a nucleus and the other joins nuclei. Nuclear fission is the splitting of a large nucleus into smaller pieces. Nuclear fusion is the joining of two nuclei, which occurs under extreme temperatures and pressures. Fusion occurs naturally in stars, and is the process responsible for the release of great amounts of energy. When fusion occurs, many atomic nuclei with like charges are joined together, forming a heavier nucleus. When this occurs, energy can be absorbed and/or released.

Periodic Table

The periodic table groups elements with similar chemical properties together. The grouping of elements is based on atomic structure. It shows periodic trends of physical and chemical properties and identifies families of elements with similar properties. It is a common model for organizing and understanding elements. In the periodic table, each element has its own cell that includes varying amounts of information presented in symbol form about the properties of the element. Cells in the table are arranged in rows (periods) and columns (groups or families). At minimum, a cell includes the symbol for the element and its atomic number. The cell for hydrogen, for example, which appears first in the upper left corner, includes an "H" and a "1" above the letter. Elements are ordered by atomic number, left to right, top to bottom.

In the periodic table, the groups are the columns numbered 1 through 18 that group elements with similar outer electron shell configurations. Since the configuration of the outer electron shell is one of the primary factors affecting an element's chemical properties, elements within the same group have similar chemical properties. Previous naming conventions for groups have included the use of Roman numerals and upper-case letters. Currently, the periodic table groups are: Group 1, alkali metals; Group 2, alkaline earth metals; Groups 3-12, transition metals; Group 13, boron family; Group 14; carbon family; Group 15, pnictogens; Group 16, chalcogens; Group 17, halogens; Group 18, noble gases.

In the periodic table, there are seven periods (rows), and within each period there are blocks that group elements with the same outer electron subshell (more on this in the next section). The number of electrons in that outer shell determines which group an element belongs to within a given block. Each row's number (1, 2, 3, etc.) corresponds to the highest number electron shell that is in use. For example, row 2 uses only electron shells 1 and 2, while row 7 uses all shells from 1-7.

Atomic radii will decrease from left to right across a period (row) on the periodic table. In a group (column), there is an increase in the atomic radii of elements from top to bottom. Ionic radii will be smaller than the atomic radii for metals, but the opposite is true for non-metals. From left to right, electronegativity, or an atom's likeliness of taking another atom's electrons, increases. In a group, electronegativity decreases from top to bottom. Ionization energy or the amount of energy needed to get rid of an atom's outermost electron, increases across a period and decreases down a group. Electron affinity will become more negative across a period but will not change much within a group. The melting point decreases from top to bottom in the metal groups and increases from top to bottom in the non-metal groups.

Electronegativity is a measure of how capable an atom is of attracting a pair of bonding electrons. It refers to the fact that one atom exerts slightly more force in a bond than another, creating a dipole. If the electronegative difference between two atoms is small, the atoms will form a polar covalent bond. If the difference is large, the atoms will form an ionic bond. When there is no electronegativity, a pure nonpolar covalent bond is formed. Electronegativity can be discussed as a trend in the periodic table. Fluorine (F) has the greatest electronegativity, and elements to the left and below fluorine have lower levels of electronegativity. This property of elements is often measured using the Pauling scale, which ranges from 4.0 (fluorine) to 0.7 (francium). Elements with high electronegativity are highly reactive because they can capture electrons. The symbols δ^+ (delta plus) and δ^- (delta minus) stand for fractional charges.

Ionization energy is the energy required for an electron to free itself from the grip of its neutral atom. Ionization energy increases across a row. Groups on the left of the table have fewer valence electrons and noble gases have the maximum number of valence electrons (a filled outer shell). Ionization energy can be measured in kilojoules (kJ) per mole or electron volts (eV) per atom (1 kJ/mol = 0.010364 eV/atom). Elements with low ionization energies are highly reactive because they can easily give up electrons.

Electrons

Electrons are subatomic particles that orbit the nucleus at various levels commonly referred to as layers, shells, or clouds. The orbiting electron or electrons account for only a fraction of the atom's mass. They are much smaller than the nucleus, are negatively charged, and exhibit wave-like characteristics. Electrons are part of the lepton family of elementary particles. Electrons can occupy orbits that are varying distances away from the nucleus, and tend to occupy the lowest energy level they can. If an atom has all its electrons in the lowest available positions, it has a stable electron arrangement. The outermost electron shell of an atom in its uncombined state is known as the valence shell. The electrons there are called valence electrons, and it is their number that determines bonding behavior. Atoms tend to react in a manner that will allow them to fill or empty their valence shells.

Chemical bonds involve a negative-positive attraction between an electron or electrons and the nucleus of an atom or nuclei of more than one atom. The attraction keeps the atom cohesive, but also enables the formation of bonds among other atoms and molecules. Each of the seven energy levels (or shells) of an atom has a maximum number of electrons it can contain. The farther away from the nucleus an electron is, the more energy it has. The first shell, or K-shell, holds a maximum of 2 electrons; the second, L, holds 8; the third, M, holds 18; the fourth, N, holds 32; the fifth, O, holds 60; the sixth, P, holds 82; the seventh, Q, holds 108. The shells also have subshells. Chemical bonds form and break between atoms when atoms gain, lose, or share an electron in the outer (valence) shell. Polar bond refers to a covalent type of bond with a separation of charge. One end is negative and the other is positive. The hydrogen-oxygen bond in water is one example of a polar bond.

There are seven electron shells. One is closest to the nucleus and seven is the farthest away. Electron shells can also be identified with the letters K, L, M, N, O, P, and Q. Traditionally, there were four subshells identified by the first letter of their descriptive name: s (sharp), p (principal), d (diffuse), and f (fundamental). The maximum number of electrons for each subshell is as follows: s is 2, p is 6, d is 10, and f is 14. Every shell has an s subshell, the second shell and those above also have a p subshell, the third shell and those above also have a d subshell, and so on. Each subshell contains atomic orbitals, which describes the wave-like characteristics of an electron or a pair of electrons expressed as two angles and the distance from the nucleus. Atomic orbital is a concept used to express the likelihood of an electron's position in accordance with the idea of wave-particle duality.

Electron configuration: This is a trend whereby electrons fill shells and subshells in an element in a particular order and with a particular number of electrons. The chemical properties of the elements reflect their electron configurations. Energy levels (shells) do not have to be completely filled before the next one begins to be filled. An example of electron configuration notation is $1s^2 2s^2 2p^5$, where the first number is the row (period), or shell. The letter refers to the subshell of the shell, and the number in superscript is the number of electrons in the subshell. A common shorthand method for electron configuration notation is to use a noble gas (in a bracket) to abbreviate the shells that elements have in common. For example, the electron configuration for neon is $1s^2 2s^2 2p^6$. The configuration for phosphorus is $1s^2 2s^2 2p^6 3s^2 3p^3$, which can be written as $[Ne]3s^2 3p^3$. Subshells are filled in the following manner: 1s, 2s, 2p, 3s, 3p, 4s, 3d, 4p, 5s, 4d, 5p, 6s, 4f, 5d, 6p, 7s, 5f, 6d, and 7p.

Most atoms are neutral since the positive charge of the protons in the nucleus is balanced by the negative charge of the surrounding electrons. Electrons are transferred between atoms when they come into contact with each other. This creates a molecule or atom in which the number of electrons does not equal the number of protons, which gives it a positive or negative charge. A negative ion is created when an atom gains electrons, while a positive ion is created when an atom loses electrons. An ionic bond is formed between ions with opposite charges. The resulting compound is neutral. Ionization refers to the process by which neutral particles are ionized into charged particles. Gases and plasmas can be partially or fully ionized through ionization.

Atoms interact by transferring or sharing the electrons furthest from the nucleus. Known as the outer or valence electrons, they are responsible for the chemical properties of an element. Bonds between atoms are created when electrons are paired up by being transferred or shared. If electrons are transferred from one atom to another, the bond is ionic. If electrons are shared, the bond is covalent. Atoms of the same element may bond together to form molecules or crystalline solids. When two or more different types of atoms bind together chemically, a compound is made. The physical properties of compounds reflect the nature of the interactions among their molecules. These interactions are determined by the structure of the molecule, including the atoms they consist of and the distances and angles between them.

Isotopes and Molecules

The number of protons in an atom determines the element of that atom. For instance, all helium atoms have exactly two protons, and all oxygen atoms have exactly eight protons. If two atoms have the same number of protons, then they are the same element. However, the number of neutrons in two atoms can be different without the atoms being different elements. Isotope is the term used to distinguish between atoms that have the same number of protons but a different number of neutrons. The names of isotopes have the element name with the mass number. Recall that the mass number is the number of protons plus the number of neutrons. For example, carbon-12 refers to an atom that has 6 protons, which makes it carbon, and 6 neutrons. In other words, 6 protons + 6 neutrons = 12. Carbon-13 has six protons and seven neutrons, and carbon-14 has six protons and eight neutrons. Isotopes can also be written with the mass number in superscript before the element symbol. For example, carbon-12 can be written as ^{12}C.

The important properties of water (H_2O) are high polarity, hydrogen bonding, cohesiveness, adhesiveness, high specific heat, high latent heat, and high heat of vaporization. It is essential to life as we know it, as water is one of the main if not the main constituent of many living things. Water is a liquid at room temperature. The high specific heat of water means it resists the breaking of its hydrogen bonds and resists heat and motion, which is why it has a relatively high boiling point and high vaporization point. It also resists temperature change. Water is peculiar in that its solid state floats in its liquid state. Most substances are denser in their solid forms. Water is cohesive, which means it is attracted to itself. It is also adhesive, which means it readily attracts other molecules. If water tends to adhere to another substance, the substance is said to be hydrophilic. Water makes a good solvent. Substances, particularly those with polar ions and molecules, readily dissolve in water.

Electrons in an atom can orbit different levels around the nucleus. They can absorb or release energy, which can change the location of their orbit or even allow them to break free from the atom. The outermost layer is the valence layer, which contains the valence electrons. The valence layer tends to have or share eight electrons. Molecules are formed by a chemical bond between atoms, a bond which occurs at the valence level. Two basic types of bonds are covalent and ionic. A covalent bond is formed when atoms share electrons. An ionic bond is formed when an atom transfers an electron to another atom. A hydrogen bond is a weak bond between a hydrogen atom of one molecule and an electronegative atom (such as nitrogen, oxygen, or fluorine) of another molecule. The Van der Waals force is a weak force between molecules. This type of force is much weaker than actual chemical bonds between atoms.